MY LARGER EDUCATION

CLASSICS IN BLACK STUDIES

MY LARGER EDUCATION
Chapters from My Experience

Booker T. Washington

WITH AN INTRODUCTION BY
Howard McGary

Humanity Books

an imprint of Prometheus Books
59 John Glenn Drive, Amherst, New York 14228-2197

Cover image: From the *Dictionary of American Portraits,*
Dover Publications Inc., 1967.

Published by Humanity Books, an imprint of Prometheus Books

Inquiries should be addressed to
Humanity Books, 59 John Glenn Drive, Amherst, New York 14228–2197
VOICE: 716–691–0133, ext. 207; FAX: 716–564–2711
WWW.PROMETHEUSBOOKS.COM

08 07 06 05 04   5 4 3 2 1

Library of Congress Cataloging-in-Publication Data

Washington, Booker T., 1856–1915.
    My larger education : chapters from my experience / Booker T.
Washington ; with an introduction by Howard McGary.
        p. cm. — (Classics in Black studies)
    Previously published: 1911.
    Includes bibliographical references.
    ISBN 1-59102-263-0 (pbk. : alk. paper)
    1. Washington, Booker T., 1856–1915. 2. African Americans—
Biography. 3. Educators—United States—Biography. I. Title. II. Series.

E185.97.W4A3 2004
370'.92—dc22

                                                              2004013540

Printed in the United States of America on acid-free paper

E ducator and reformer BOOKER TALIAFERRO WASH-INGTON was born in Franklin County, Virginia, on April 5, 1856, the son of slave Jane Burroughs, a plantation cook, and a White father. After the Civil War, he and his mother moved to Malden, West Virginia, to join Washington Ferguson, whom his mother had married during the war. Young Booker worked at a salt furnace and then a coalmine, studying nights with the teacher of the local Black school.

In 1872 Washington enrolled at the Hampton Normal and Agricultural Institute in Hampton, Virginia, which had been chartered in 1870 as one of the first colleges for Blacks. It was also a pioneering institute in educating Native Americans. After graduating in 1875, he taught in Malden, West Virginia; studied at Wayland Seminary, Washington, DC (1878–79); and then joined the staff of Hampton. In 1881 Washington became head of Tuskegee Normal and Industrial Institute, in Alabama, and oversaw its growth as a major university for Blacks.

Washington was the most influential spokesperson for Black Americans between 1895 and 1915. He advised US presidents on racial issues and the appointment of Blacks to government positions. He received honorary degrees from Harvard University in 1896 and Dartmouth College in 1901. Washington authored a dozen books, including *The Story of My Life and Work* (1900), *Up from Slavery* (1901), *Working with the Hands* (1904), *Tuskegee and Its People: Their Ideals and Achievements* (1905), *Frederick Douglass* (1907), and *My Larger Education* (1910).

Washington died on November 14, 1915, at Tuskegee, Alabama.

INTRODUCTION

It seemed to me a great hardship that I was born poor, and it seemed an even greater hardship that I should have been born a Negro. I did not like to admit, even to myself, that I felt this way about the matter, because it seemed to me an indication of weakness and cowardice for any man to complain about the condition he was born to. Later I came to the conclusion that it was not only weak and cowardly, but that it was a mistake to think of the matter in the way in which I had done. I came to see that, along with the disadvantages, the Negro in America had some advantages, and I made up in my mind that opportunities that had been denied him from without could be more than made up by greater concentration and power within.

Booker T. Washington
(chapter 1 of *My Larger Education*)

Born a slave in 1856, in Hales Ford, Virginia, Booker T. Washington went on to become the most influential voice for racial uplift of African Americans at the beginning of the twentieth century. After emancipation in 1865, Washington and his mother moved to West Virginia. There

7

he was employed as a miner and houseboy while obtaining a modest education. He gradually earned enough money doing industrial work to finance his education at the Hampton Normal and Industrial School in Virginia. It was there that he acquired the training that qualified him for teaching. The Hampton years were crucial in Washington's development. At Hampton, he was strongly influenced by the social philosophy of Hampton's founder, Gen. Samuel Chapman Armstrong. Armstrong combined a puritan ethics with the Spartan rigor of army life. All or most commentators agree that Washington's Hampton experience had a profound impact on his life and philosophy.

Washington is probably best known for being the founder and head of Tuskegee Institute, which began as the Tuskegee Normal and Agricultural Institute in 1881. This institute has been both condemned and praised for its mission of providing an industrial education for Negroes. Washington was not ashamed to say that no time would be wasted on dead languages and superfluous studies at Tuskegee. At Tuskegee, students were taught what was practical or necessary for being successful in life. Although Washington is well known for his work to educate Negroes in the rural South, he was also a founder of the National Negro Business League and quite active in Republican politics in the South. Washington was as much a politician as he was an educator, but he never held political office.

Washington was an institution builder as well as a prolific writer. His major works include *The Future of the Negro* (1902), *The Story of the Negro* (1909), *The Man Farthest Down* (with Robert E. Parks, 1912), and of course his widely read autobiography, *Up From Slavery* (1901). All of these are important works because they help us to understand Washington and his philosophy, but they also give us insight into some of the vexing problems that confronted African Americans in the late nineteenth and early twentieth centuries and that still persist today. Washington's *My Larger Education: Being Chapters from My Experience,* published in 1911, has not been given the attention that it deserves. This book develops several important themes that run through his earlier writings: the importance of an education that can be put to practical use; the value of integrity and self-reliance; the necessity for seeing the plight of the Negro in a larger context; the role of a free press in racial uplift; the value and compatibility of commitment to race and country; and the use of capitalistic free markets to achieve racial uplift. I strongly recommend it both to general readers and to scholars who want to learn more about Washington and his ideas, but it is also an important part of Washington's corpus that will prove useful to scholars who want to rethink how Washington has been characterized in the lay and scholarly communities.

Washington's defense of the themes mentioned above has led critics to label him an accommodationist and worse. They believe that by emphasizing industrial education over a liberal education, by putting more emphasis on personal failings rather than institutional injustices, by devaluing the necessity of protest, and by underestimating the challenges that confronted African Americans in an anti-Black racist society, Washington should not be cast in the same positive light as Frederick Douglass and W. E. B. Du Bois as champions of racial uplift. The essays in *My Larger Education* provide the reader with the opportunity to better evaluate this criticism of Washington.

Each of the twelve essays in this book, besides being of value in assessing the accuracy of characterizing Washington as an accommodationist, should be read to gain a better understanding of the specific concerns discussed in each chapter. In chapters 1 and 3, Washington discusses practical things that can be learned by being a careful observer of people and their circumstances. The pragmatics of a free press in the context of racial uplift is discussed in chapter 4. The true value of the Negro intellectual is explored in chapter 5. In chapters 2 and 6, he examines the importance of educating the Negro masses by the use of everyday experiences and real-life problems. Chapters 7, 8, 9, and 10 provide an account of what can be learned from common people, as well as economic and political leaders. Finally, in chapters 11 and 12, Washington sketches his pragmatic account of education.

Nearly one hundred years after the publication of *My Larger Education*, many African Americans still lag behind White Americans when it comes to education, wealth, and other indices of personal well-being. Some writers believe this disparity can be explained by institutional racism. Others maintain that the fault lies more with African Americans themselves. The supporters of the latter view believe, for example, that Washington's proposals for the educational advancement of African Americans are the historical antecedent of their position. In other words, the disparities can be traced to personal shortcomings rather than institutional failings. Is this reading of Washington correct?

Perhaps the most influential account of how Washington should be read can be found in Louis R. Harlan's 1972 two-volume biography of Washington and his fourteen-volume *Booker T. Washington Papers*. Professor Harlan, more than any other scholar, has painted a picture of Washington as a person who acquiesced in racial segregation, and who accepted complacently the denial of equal rights to African Americans after Reconstruction. The debate over who Washington was continues today.

In a recent article, philosopher Bill Lawson defended Washington against Harlan's characterization by placing Washington within the American pragmatist tradition (2004). According to Lawson, Washington was more interested in finding practical solutions to problems than in fitting into some theoretical construction. Washington was not interested in protesting against racial discrimination unless doing so eliminated or reduced the discrimination. He was not interested in adhering to some educational theory unless doing so helped people to learn things that could be used to make their lives better. Lawson disagrees with writers like Diane McWhorter, who argues (2001). *My Larger Education* provides support for Lawson's pragmatist reading of Washington. Washington wrote:

> My experience is that people who call themselves "The Intellectuals" understand theories, but they do not understand things. I have long been convinced that, if these men could have gone into the South and taken up and become interested in some practical work which would have brought them in touch with people and things, the whole world would have looked very different to them. Bad as conditions might have seemed at first, when they saw that actual progress was being made, they would have taken a more hopeful view of the situation. (pp. 110–11)★

Lawson is not alone in his defense of Harlan's characterization of Washington. Robert J. Norrell (2003/2004) challenges the view that Washington was an obedient accommodationist chosen by Whites to maintain White supremacy. Quite to the contrary, Norrell believes that Washington fought to destroy the effects of a system of White supremacy.

★Pagination in this edition.

Most scholars who have discussed Harlan's characterization of Washington have done so in two contexts: Washington's disputes with W. E. B. Du Bois and Washington's support for Republican politics, especially in the South. These are important contexts for assessing Washington's thinking, but they are not the only contexts. Norrell suggests that when we look at Washington's writings in other historical contexts, we may reject Harlan's characterization of him. According to Norrell, a crucial context for understanding Washington is the thinking of White people about race relations at the turn of the twentieth century. Or put another way, how do we achieve racial uplift for African Americans given the prevailing images of Negroes in the minds of White people at the time? This is an interesting proposal and perhaps *My Larger Education* can be used to support a different understanding than the one popularized by Harlan and other scholars who are critical of Washington.

But perhaps the most important context for evaluating Washington's moral and political beliefs is the debate in the late nineteenth century that continues today over who should be schooled and the nature of that schooling. It is well known that Washington was an avid supporter of industrial education, but what are not clear are his reasons for doing so. Did these include a lack of appreciation for the rights of African Americans? Did he fail to see that supporting industrial education for African Americans in effect meant that they would not enjoy the same educational opportunities as White Americans? Washington seemed to think not. *In My Larger Education,* he wrote:

> The importance of the scheme of education which has
> been worked out, particularly in industrial schools, is not
> confined to America or to the Negro race. Wherever in
> Europe, in Africa, in Asia, or elsewhere great masses are

coming for the first time in contact with and under the influence of a higher civilization, the methods of industrial education that have been worked out in the South by, with, and through the Negro schools are steadily gaining recognition and importance. (p. 260)

Chapters 1, 6, 7, 11, and 12 of *My Larger Education* will provide the reader with valuable evidence in Washington's own words about his thinking on this issue.

African American neoconservatives have also challenged Harlan and McWhorter's characterizations of Washington. Neoconservative writers like Thomas Sowell and Walter Williams have adopted Washington as a hero. They have encouraged African Americans to adopt Washington's strategy of using the capitalist free market and a reliance on time-tested moral values rather than government intervention to uplift the race. But in his important book *Blacks and Social Justice* (1984), Bernard Boxill rejects the interpretation of Washington offered by Sowell and Williams. Boxill believes that Washington did not think that the free market and the proper values would be sufficient to uplift a race that was and still is victimized by a system of racial discrimination. According to Boxill, Sowell and Williams are willing to downplay the importance of the requirements of distributive and compensatory justice, but Washington, on the other hand, felt these requirements should not be ignored. Most people rely on Washington's "Atlanta Exposition Address" (1895) when they interpret what Washington had to say about demanding what is required by justice. This is an important piece of evidence, but chapter 5 of *My Larger Education*, "The Intellectuals and the Boston Mob," should definitely be consulted. Washington wrote the following about Negro leaders who emphasized rights and justice:

Mr. Douglass's great life-work had been in the political agitation that led to the destruction of slavery. He had been the great defender of the race, and in the struggle to win from Congress and from the country at large the recognition of the Negro's rights as a man and a citizen he had played an important part. But the long and bitter political struggle in which he had engaged against slavery had not prepared Mr. Douglass to take up the equally difficult task of fitting the Negro for the opportunities and responsibilities of freedom. The same was true to a large extent of other Negro leaders. At the time when I met these men and heard them speak I was invariably impressed, though young and inexperienced, that there was something lacking in their public utterances. I felt that the millions of Negroes needed something more than to be reminded of their sufferings and of their political rights; that they needed to do something more than merely to defend themselves. (p. 101)

Finally, Frederick Douglass and Booker T. Washington are both seen as ardent proponents of the racial-assimilation society. By this is meant a society where a person will be judged by the contents of his or her character rather than by his or her race. Although they both endorsed racial assimilation to different degrees, it is clear that Washington did not believe that people should deny or feel ashamed of their racial identities. Washington speaks to this point in *My Larger Education*.

The most difficult and trying of the classes of persons with which I am brought in contact is the coloured man or woman who is ashamed of his or her colour, ashamed of his or her race and, because of this fact, is always in a bad temper. I have had opportunities, such as few coloured men have had, of meeting and getting

acquainted with many of the best white people, North
and South. This has never led me to desire to get away
from my own people. On the contrary, I have always
returned to my own people and my own work with
renewed interest. (p. 57)

As an assimilationist, Washington believed that our goal
should be a society where racial identities serve to unite
rather than separate, but he did not believe that forced
assimilation would work. Where Douglass used a natural-
rights framework to judge strategies for achieving the goal
of assimilation, Washington was a strong advocate of judging
these strategies by how well they served the common good.
Washington always urged people, especially African Americans, to look at their problems in a broader context. For
example, he insisted in *My Larger Education* that the problem
of Negro education in the South should be seen as a part of
a larger problem.

Clear ideas did not come into my mind on this subject at
once. It was only gradually that I gained the notion that
there had been two races in slavery; that both were now
engaged in a struggle to adjust themselves to the new
conditions; that the progress of each meant the advancement of the other; and that anything that I attempted to
do for the members of my own race would be of no real
value to them unless it was of equal value to the members of the white race by whom they were surrounded.
(pp. 42–43)

So, in conclusion, the reprinting of Washington's *My
Larger Education* should prove to be beneficial to anyone who
wants to learn more about Washington and his ideas as well
as those readers who wish to gain insight into the problems

that African Americans faced at the turn of the twentieth century. Clearly, Washington's work has historical value, but it can also be used to engage problems that still persist today, for example, improving the quality of education in African American and minority communities. Finally, the wonderful photographs of people and places in the text really help to give the reader a better feel for the times.

Howard McGary
Department of Philosophy
Rutgers, The State University of New Jersey

References

Boxill, Bernard R. 1984. *Blacks and Social Justice.* Lanham, MD: Rowman and Allanheld.

Harlan, Louis R. 1983. *Booker T. Washington: The Wizard of Tuskegee 1901–1915.* New York: Oxford University Press.

———, ed. 1972. *The Booker T. Washington Papers.* Urbana: University of Illinois Press.

Lawson, Bill E. 2004. "A Pragmatist at Work." In *Pragmatism and the Problem of Race.* Edited by Bill E. Lawson and Donald F. Koch. Bloomington: Indiana University Press.

McWhorter, Diane. 2001. "Overcoming Repeatedly." NY Times.com review, July 29, 2001.

Norrell, Robert J. 2003/2004. "Booker T. Washington: Understanding the Wizard of Tuskegee." *Journal of Blacks in Higher Education* 42 (Winter): 96–109.

Sowell, Thomas. 1995. *Race and Culture: A World View.* New York: Harper Collins.

Washington, Booker T. (with Robert E. Parks). 1912. *The Man Farthest Down: A Record of Observation and Study in Europe.* With an introduction by St. Clair Drake. New Brunswick, NJ: Transaction Books, 1984.

————. 1911. *My Larger Education: Being Chapters from My Experience.* Garden City, NY: Doubleday, Page & Company.

————. 1909. *The Story of the Negro: The Rise of the Race from Slavery.* Gloucester, MA: P. Smith, 1969.

————. 1902. *The Future of the American Negro.* New York: American Library, 1969.

————. 1900. *Up from Slavery.* Norwood, MA: Norwood Press.

————. 1895. "The Atlanta Exposition Address." In *Negro Social and Political Thought 1850–1920.* Edited by Howard Brotz. New York: Basic Books, 1966.

Williams, Walter. 1982. *The State Against Blacks.* New York: McGraw-Hill.

MY LARGER
EDUCATION

A NEW PORTRAIT OF MR. WASHINGTON

"When I had something to say about the white people I said it to the white people;
when I had something to say about coloured people I said it to coloured people."

CONTENTS

I. Learning from Men and Things   23

II. Building a School around a Problem   37

III. Some Exceptional Men, and
What I Have Learned from Them   59

IV. My Experience with Reporters
and Newspapers   81

V. The Intellectuals and the Boston Mob   97

VI. A Commencement Oration on Cabbages   117

VII. Colonel Roosevelt and
What I Have Learned from Him   141

VIII. My Educational Campaigns Through
the South and What They Taught Me   159

IX. What I Have Learned from Black Men   177

X. Meeting High and Low in Europe 203

XI. What I Learned About Education
in Denmark 221

XII. The Mistakes and the Future of
Negro Education 241

I

LEARNING FROM MEN AND THINGS

I T HAS been my fortune to be associated all my life with a problem—a hard, perplexing, but important problem. There was a time when I looked upon this fact as a great misfortune. It seemed to me a great hardship that I was born poor, and it seemed an even greater hardship that I should have been born a Negro. I did not like to admit, even to myself, that I felt this way about the matter, because it seemed to me an indication of weakness and cowardice for any man to complain about the condition he was born to. Later I came to the conclusion that it was not only weak and cowardly, but that it was a mistake to think of the matter in the way in which I had done. I came to see that, along with his disadvantages, the Negro in America had some advantages, and I made up my mind that opportunities that had been denied him from without could be more than made up by greater concentration and power within.

Perhaps I can illustrate what I mean by a fact I learned while I was in school. I recall my teacher's explaining to the class one day how it was that steam or any other form of energy, if allowed to escape and dissipate itself, loses its value as a motive power. Energy must be confined; steam must be locked in a boiler in order to generate power. The same thing seems to have been true in the case of the Negro. Where the Negro has met with discriminations and with difficulties because of his race, he has invariably tended to get up more steam. When this steam has been rightly directed and controlled, it has become a great force in the upbuilding of the race. If, on the contrary, it merely spent itself in fruitless agitation and hot air, no good has come of it.

Paradoxical as it may seem, the difficulties that the Negro has met since emancipation have, in my opinion, not always, but on the whole, helped him more than they have hindered him. For example, I think the progress which the Negro has made within less than half a century in the matter of learning to read and write the English language has been due in large part to the fact that, in slavery, this knowledge was forbidden him. My experience and observation have taught me that people who try to withhold the best things in civilization from any group of people, or race of people, not infrequently aid that people to the very things that they are trying to withhold from them. I am sure that, in my own case, I should never have made the efforts that I did make in my early boyhood to get an education and still later to develop the Tuskegee Institute in Alabama if I had not been conscious of the fact that there were a large number of people in the world who did not believe that the Negro boy could learn or that members of the Negro race could build up and conduct a large institution of learning.

A wider acquaintance with men in all the different grades of life taught me that the Negro's case is not peculiar. The majority of successful men are persons who have had difficulties to overcome, problems to master; and, in overcoming those difficulties and mastering those problems, they have gained strength of mind and a clearness of vision that few persons who have lived a life of ease have been able to attain. Experience has taught me, in fact, that no man should be pitied because, every day in his life, he faces a hard, stubborn problem, but rather that it is the man who has no problem to solve, no hardships to face, who is to be pitied.

His misfortune consists in the fact that he has nothing in his life which will strengthen and form his character; nothing to call out his latent powers, and deepen and widen his hold on life. It has come home to me more in recent years that I have had, just because my life has been connected with a problem, some unusual opportunities. I have had unusual opportunities for example in getting an education in the broader sense of the word.

If I had not been born a slave, for example, I never could have had the opportunity, perhaps, of associating day by day with the most ignorant people, so far as books are concerned, and thus coming in contact with people of this class at first hand. The most fortunate part of my early experience was that which gave me the opportunity of getting into direct contact and of communing with and taking lessons from the old class of coloured people who have been slaves. At the present time few experiences afford me more genuine pleasure than to get a day or a half a day off and go out into the country, miles from town and railroad, and spend the time in close contact with a coloured farmer and his family.

And then I have felt for a long while that, if I had not been a slave and lived on a slave plantation, I never would have had the opportunity to learn nature, to love the soil, to love cows and pigs and trees and flowers and birds and worms and creeping things. I have always been intensely fond of outdoor life. Perhaps the explanation for this lies partly in the fact that I was born nearly out of doors. I have also, from my earliest childhood, been very fond of animals and fowls. When I was but a child, and a slave, I had close and interesting acquaintances with animals.

During my childhood days, as a slave, I did not see very much of my mother, since she was obliged to leave her children very early in the morning to begin her day's work. The early departure of my mother often made the matter of my securing breakfast uncertain. This led to my first intimate acquaintance with animals.

In those days it was the custom upon the plantation to boil the Indian corn that was fed to the cows and pigs. At times, when I had failed to get any other breakfast, I used to go to the places where the cows and pigs were fed and make my breakfast off this boiled corn, or else go to the place where it was the custom to boil the corn, and get my share there before it was taken to the animals.

If I was not there at the exact moment of feeding, I could still find enough corn scattered around the fence or the trough to satisfy me. Some people may think that this was a pretty bad way in which to get one's food, but, leaving out the name and the associations, there was nothing very bad about it. Any one who has eaten hard-boiled corn knows it has a delicious taste. I never pass a pot of boiled corn now without yielding to the temptation to eat a few grains.

I think that I owe a great deal of my present strength and ability to work to my love of out-door life. It is true that the amount of time that I can spend in the open air is now very limited. Taken on an average, it is perhaps not more than an hour a day, but I make the most of that hour. In addition to this I get much pleasure out of the anticipation and the planning for that hour.

When I am at my home at Tuskegee, I usually find a way, by rising early in the morning, to spend at least half an hour in my garden, or with my fowls, pigs, or cows. As far as I can get the time, I like to find the new eggs each morning myself, and when at home am selfish enough to permit no one else to do this in my place. As with the growing plants, there is a sense of freshness and newness and of restfulness in connection with the finding and handling of newly laid eggs that is delightful to me. Both the anticipation and the realization are most pleasing. I begin the day by seeing how many eggs I can find, or how many little chickens there are that are just beginning to peep through the shells.

I am deeply interested in the different kinds of fowls, and, aside from the large number grown by the school in its poultry house and yards, I grow at my own home common chickens, Plymouth Rocks, Buff Cochins and Brahmas, Peking ducks, and fan-tailed pigeons.

The pig, I think, is my favourite animal. I do not know how this will strike the taste of my readers, but it is true. In addition to some common bred pigs, I keep a few Berkshires and some Poland Chinas; and it is a real pleasure to me to watch their development and increase from month to month. Practically all the pork used in my family is of my own raising.

This will, perhaps, illustrate what I mean when I say that I have gotten a large part of my education from actual contact with things, rather than through the medium of books. I like to touch things and handle them; I like to watch plants grow and observe the behaviour of animals. For the same reason, I like to deal with things, as far as possible, at first hand, in the way that the carpenter deals with wood, the blacksmith with iron, and the farmer with the earth. I believe that there is something gained by getting acquainted,

A PARTIAL VIEW OF HAMPTON INSTITUTE, VIRGINIA

Where Mr. Washington received a large part of the training
and of the inspiration for his great work

in the way which I have described, with the physical world about you that is almost indispensable.

A number of years ago, in a book called, "Up From Slavery," I told a story of my early life, describing the manner in which I got my early schooling and the circumstances under which I came to start the Tuskegee Normal and Industrial Institute. At the time that school was organized I had read very little, and, in fact, few books on the subject of teaching, and knew very little about the science of education and pedagogy. I had had the advantage of going through an exceptional school at Hampton and of coming in contact with an inspired teacher in General Armstrong; but I had never attempted to formulate the methods of teaching I used in that school, and I had very little experience in applying them to the new and difficult problems I met as soon as I attempted to conduct a school of my own. What I learned about the science of education I learned in

my efforts in working out the plans for, and organizing and
perfecting the educational methods at, Tuskegee.

The necessity of collecting large sums of money every
year to carry on the work at Tuskegee compelled me to
travel much and brought me in contact with all kinds of
people. As soon as I began to meet educated and cultivated
people, people who had had the advantage of study in
higher institutions of learning, as well as the advantages of
much reading and travel, I soon became conscious of my
own disadvantages. I found that the people I met were able
to speak fluently and with perfect familiarity about a great
many things with which I was acquainted in only the
vaguest sort of way. In speaking they used words and phrases
from authors whom I had never read and often never heard
of. All this made me feel more keenly my deficiencies, and
the more I thought about it the more it troubled and wor-
ried me. It made me feel all the more badly because I discovered that, if I were to carry on the work I had undertaken to do, if I was ever going to accomplish any of the
things that it seemed to me important to do, I should never
find time, no matter how diligent and studious I might be,
to overtake them and possess myself of the knowledge and
familiarity with books for which I envied those persons
who had been more highly educated than myself.

After a time, however, I found that while I was at a certain disadvantage among highly educated and cultivated
people in certain directions, I had certain advantages over
them in others. I found that the man who has an intimate
acquaintance with some department of life through personal
experience has a great advantage over persons who have
gained their knowledge of life almost entirely through
books. I found also that, by using my personal experience
and observation; by making use of the stories that I had

heard, as illustrations; by relating some incident that happened in my own case or some incident that I had heard from some one else, I could frequently express what I had to say in a much clearer and more impressive way than if I made use of the language of books or the statements and quotations from the authors of books. More than that, as I reflected upon the matter, I discovered that these authors, in their books, were after all merely making use of their own experiences or expressing ideas which they had worked out in actual life, and that to make use of their language and ideas was merely to get life second hand.

The result was that I made up my mind that I would try to make up for my defects in my knowledge of books by my knowledge of men and things. I said I would take living men and women for my study, and I would give the closest attention possible to everything that was going on in the world about me. I determined that I would get my education out of my work; I would learn about education in solving the problems of the school as they arose from day to day, and learn about life by learning to deal with men. I said to myself that I would try to learn something from every man I met; make him my text-book, read him, study him, and learn something from him. So I began deliberately to try to learn from men. I learned something from big men and something from little men, from the man with prejudice and the man without prejudice. As I studied and understood them, I found that I began to like men better; even those who treated me badly did not cause me to lose my temper or patience, as soon as I found that I could learn something from them.

For example, some years ago, I had an experience which taught me a lesson in politeness and liberality which I shall long remember. I was in a large city making calls on wealthy people in order to interest them in our work at Tuskegee Institute. I called at the office of a man, and he spoke to me in the most abrupt and insulting manner. He not only refused to give any money but spoke of my race in a manner that no gentleman of culture ought ever to permit himself to speak of another race. A few minutes later I called on another gentleman in the same city, who received me politely, thanked me for calling upon him, but explained that he was so situated that he could not help me. My interview with the first man occupied about twice as much of his time and my time as was true of the second gentleman. I learned from this experience that it takes no more time to be polite to every one than it does to be rude.

During the later years of my experience I have had the good fortune to study not only white men and learn from them, but coloured men as well. In my earlier experiences I used to have sympathy with the coloured people who were narrow and bitter toward white people. As I grew older I began to study that class of coloured people, and I found that they did not get anywhere, that their bitterness and narrowness toward the white man did not hurt the white man or change his feeling toward the coloured race, but that, in almost every case, the cherishing of such feeling toward the white man reacted upon the coloured man and made him narrow and bitter.

In the chapters which follow, I have given some account of the way in which my work has brought me in contact, not so much with plants and animals and with physical objects, but rather with human institutions, with politics, with newspapers, with educational and social problems of various kinds and descriptions, and I have tried to indicate in every case the way in which I have been educated through them.

One of the purposes in writing these later chapters from my experience is to complete the story of my education which I began in the book, "Up From Slavery"; to answer the questions I have frequently been asked as to how I have worked out for myself the educational methods which we are now using at Tuskegee; and, finally, to illustrate, for the benefit of the members of my own race, some of the ways in which a people who are struggling upward may turn disadvantages into opportunities; how they may gain within themselves something that will compensate them for what they have been deprived of from without.

If I have learned much from things, I have learned more from men. The work that I started to do brought me early in contact with some of the most generous, high-minded and public-spirited persons in the country. In the chapters that follow I have tried to indicate what I have learned from contact with those men. Perhaps I can best indicate the way in which I have been educated by my contact with these men if I tell something of my relations with one man from whom, after General Armstrong, my first teacher, I learned, perhaps, more than from any other. I refer to the late William H. Baldwin, Jr.

I well remember my first meeting with Mr. Baldwin, although the exact date has now slipped from my memory. He was at that time manager and vice-president of the Southern Railway, with headquarters in Washington, D.C. I had been given a letter to him by his father, in Boston. I found him one morning in his office and presented this letter, which he read over carefully, as was his custom in such matters. Then we began talking about the school at Tuskegee and its work. I had been in the room but a few minutes when the conviction forced itself upon me that I had met a man who could thoroughly understand me and whom I understood. Indeed, I had the feeling that I was in the presence of one in whose mind there was neither faltering nor concealment, and one from whom it would be impossible to hide a single thought or purpose. I never had occasion, during all the years that I knew Mr. Baldwin, to change the opinion formed of him at my first visit, or to feel that the understanding established between us then was ever clouded or diminished.

Mr. Baldwin did not at first manifest any definite interest in the work at Tuskegee. He said he would come down and "look us over" and if he found we were doing "the real thing," as he expressed it, he would do anything he could to help us.

Within a few weeks after this first meeting, Mr. Baldwin fulfilled his promise to "look us over" and see if we were doing "the real thing." He spent a busy day on the grounds of the institution, going through every department with the thoroughness of an experienced executive. He found, as a matter of course, a great many deficiencies in the details of the management and organization of the school, but he saw what the institution was striving to do and at once determined to help. In fact, from that time he never lost an opportunity to serve the institution in every possible way. He was just as deeply and as practically interested in everything that concerned the progress and reputation of the school and its work as any one connected with it. I think I never met any one who was more genuinely interested than Mr. Baldwin in the success of the Negro people. During his last visit to Tuskegee I remember that Mrs. Washington said to me one day that she would be glad when he went away. She meant that he sympathized too deeply, felt too profoundly the bigness of the task and the limitations under which the school was labouring. He was touched by everything he saw. The struggles of individual students and teachers whom he came to know weighed heavily on him and he needed to get out of the atmosphere of the school and its work, and rest. None of us realized at that time that the disease that finally took him away was already doing its fatal work.

William H. Baldwin, Jr., understood, as few men have, the Negro people, and, understanding them as he did, he was in full sympathy with their ambition to rise to a position of usefulness as large and as honourable as that of any other race. Persons who knew him only slightly, after hearing him express himself on the race question, gained the impression that he was not in full sympathy with the deepest aspirations of the Negro people. But this impression was mistaken. He was, before all, anxious that the Negro people, in their struggle to go forward and succeed, should not mistake the appearance for the real thing. In his effort to have them avoid this danger he sometimes seemed to go too far.

But I would do injustice to the memory of Mr. Baldwin if, by anything I have written or said, I should leave the impression that, because he was interested in the welfare of the Negro, he was any the less interested in the progress of the white race in the South. He saw with perfect clearness that both races were, to a certain extent, hampered in their struggles upward by conditions which they had inherited and for which neither was wholly responsible. He saw, also, that in the long run the welfare of each was bound up with that of the other. Much as he did for Negro education, he never overlooked an opportunity to get money and secure support for the education of the unfortunate white people of the South.

Mr. Baldwin's greatest service to Tuskegee Institute was in the reorganization of the finances of the institution. When he first became one of the trustees, the business organization of the school, its finances, and the system of keeping the accounts were in a very uncertain and unsatisfactory condition. He began at once to look into our investments and to study the items of our annual budget. The school was growing rapidly. The number of productive industries carried on by the school, the large amount of building we were engaged in, and the large amount of business carried on between the different departments made the accounts of the school particularly complicated and the problem of a proper business organization a most important one.

As I look back over the years in which he and I worked together, it seems to me that the most pleasant and profitable hours I have ever known were spent with Mr. Baldwin in his library in Brooklyn, while we studied out together the problems and discussed the questions which this work involved. When I came to New York he would often invite me to his home and, as soon as dinner was over, we would spend three or four hours in his library, sometimes not breaking up our conference until after midnight.

Among other things I learned from Mr. Baldwin was that it is the smaller, the petty, things in life that divide people. It is the great tasks that bring men together. Any man who will take up his life in a broad spirit, not of class nor sect nor locality, but in the freer spirit which seeks to perform a work simply because it is good, that man can have the support and the friendship of the best and highest people in the world.

As I have said before, I do not regret that I was born a slave. I am not sorry that I found myself part of a problem; on the contrary, that problem has given direction and meaning to my life and has brought me friendships and comforts that I could have gotten in no other way.

II BUILDING A SCHOOL AROUND A PROBLEM

ONE of the first questions that I had to answer for myself after beginning my work at Tuskegee was how I was to deal with public opinion on the race question.

It may seem strange that a man who had started out with the humble purpose of establishing a little Negro industrial school in a small Southern country town should find himself, to any great extent, either helped or hindered in his work by what the general public was thinking and saying about any of the large social or educational problems of the day. But such was the case at that time in Alabama; and so it was that I had not gone very far in my work before I found myself trying to formulate clear and definite answers to some very fundamental questions.

The questions came to me in this way: Coloured people wanted to know why I proposed to teach their children to work. They said that they and their parents had been compelled to work for two hundred and fifty years, and now they wanted their children to go to school so that they might be free and live like the white folks—without working. That was the way in which the average coloured man looked at the matter.

THE SITE OF TUSKEGEE INSTITUTE WHEN IT WAS FIRST BOUGHT

Two of the buildings are still in use as dormitories

Some of the Southern white people, on the contrary, were opposed to any kind of education of the Negro. Others inquired whether I was merely going to train preachers and teachers, or whether I proposed to furnish them with trained servants.

Some of the people in the North understood that I proposed to train the Negro to be a mere "hewer of wood and drawer of water," and feared that my school would make no effort to prepare him to take his place in the community as a man and a citizen.

Of course all these different views about the kind of education that the Negro ought or ought not to have were deeply tinged with racial and sectional feelings. The rule of the "carpet-bag" government had just come to an end in Alabama. The masses of the white people were very bitter against the Negroes as a result of the excitement and agitation of the Reconstruction period.

On the other hand, the coloured people—who had recently lost, to a very large extent, their place in the politics of the state—were greatly discouraged and disheartened. Many of them feared that they were going to be drawn back into slavery. At this time also there was still a great deal of bitterness between the North and the South in regard to anything that concerned political matters.

I found myself, as it were, at the angle where these opposing forces met. I saw that, in carrying out the work I had planned, I was likely to be opposed or criticised at some point by each of these parties. On the other hand, I saw just as clearly that in order to succeed I must in some way secure the support and sympathy of each of them. I knew, for example, that the South was poor and the North was rich. I knew that Northern people believed, as the South at that time did not believe, in the power of education to inspire, to uplift, and to regenerate the masses of the people. I knew that the North was eager to go forward and complete, with the aid of education, the work of liberation which had been begun with the sword, and that Northern people would be willing and glad to give their support to any school or other agency that proposed to do this work in a really fundamental way.

It was, at the same time, plain to me that no effort put forth in behalf of the members of my own race who were in the South was going to succeed unless it finally won the sympathy and support of the best white people in the South. I knew also—what many Northern people did not know or understand—that however much they might doubt the wisdom of educating the Negro, deep down in their hearts the Southern white people had a feeling of gratitude toward the Negro race; and I was convinced that in the long run any sound and sincere effort that was made to help the Negro was going to have the Southern white man's support.

Finally, I had faith in the good common-sense of the masses of my own race. I felt confident that, if I were actually on the right track in the kind of education that I proposed to give them and at the same time remained honest and sincere in all my dealings with them, I was bound to win their support, not only for the school that I had started, but for all that I had in my mind to do for them.

Still it was often a puzzling and a trying problem to determine how best to win and hold the respect of all three of these classes of people, each of which looked with such different eyes and from such widely different points of view at what I was attempting to do. The temptation which presented itself to me in my dealings with these three classes of people was to show each group the side of the subject that it would be most willing to look at, and, at the same time, to keep silent about those matters in regard to which they were likely to differ with me. There was the temptation to say to the white man the thing that the white man wanted to hear; to say to the coloured man the thing that he wanted to hear; to say one thing in the North and another in the South.

Perhaps I should have yielded to this temptation if I had not perceived that in the long run I should be found out, and that if I hoped to do anything of lasting value for my own people or for the South I must first get down to bedrock.

There is a story of an old coloured minister, which I am fond of telling, that illustrates what I mean. The old fellow was trying to explain to a Sunday-school class how it was and why it was that Pharaoh and his party were drowned when they were trying to cross the Red Sea, and how it was and why it was that the Children of Israel crossed over dry-shod. He explained it in this wise:

"When the first party came along it was early in the

morning and the ice was hard and thick, and the first party had no trouble in crossing over on the ice; but when Pharaoh and his party came along the sun was shining on the ice, and when they got on the ice it broke, and they went in and got drowned."

Now there happened to be in this class a young coloured man who had had considerable schooling, and this young fellow turned to the old minister and said:

"Now, Mr. Minister, I do not understand that kind of explanation. I have been going to school and have been studying all these conditions, and my geography teaches me that ice does not freeze within a certain distance of the equator."

The old minister replied: "Now, I'se been expecting something just like this. There's always some fellow ready to spile all the theology. The time I'se talkin' about was before they had any jogerphies or 'quaters either."

Now this old man, in his plain and simple way, was trying to brush aside all artificiality and to get down to bedrock. So it was with me. There have always been a number of educated and clever persons among my race who are able to make plausible and fine-sounding statements about all the different phases of the Negro problem, but I saw clearly that I should have to follow the example of the old preacher and start on a solid basis in order to succeed in the work that I had undertaken. So, after thinking the matter all out as I have described, I made up my mind definitely on one or two fundamental points. I determined:

First, that I should at all times be perfectly frank and honest in dealing with each of the three classes of people that I have mentioned;

Second, that I should not depend upon any "short-cuts" or expedients merely for the sake of gaining temporary popularity or advantage, whether for the time being such action brought me popularity or the reverse. With these two points clear before me as my creed, I began going forward.

One thing which gave me faith at the outset, and increased my confidence as I went on, was the insight which I early gained into the actual relations of the races in the South. I observed, in the first place, that as a result of two hundred and fifty years of slavery the two races had become bound together in intimate ways that people outside of the South could not understand, and of which the white people and coloured people themselves were perhaps not fully conscious. More than that, I perceived that the two races needed each other and that for many years to come no other labouring class of people would be able to fill the place occupied by the Negro in the life of the Southern white man.

I saw also one change that had been brought about as a result of freedom, a change which many Southern white men had, it seemed to me, failed to see. As long as slavery existed, the white man, for his own protection and in order to keep the Negro contented with his condition of servitude, was compelled to keep him in ignorance. In freedom, however, just the reverse condition exists. Now the white man is not only free to assist the Negro in his effort to rise, but he has every motive of self-interest to do so, since to uplift and educate the Negro would reduce the number of paupers and criminals of the race and increase the number and efficiency of its skilled labourers.

Clear ideas did not come into my mind on this subject at once. It was only gradually that I gained the notion that there had been two races in slavery; that both were now engaged in a struggle to adjust themselves to the new conditions; that the progress of each meant the advancement of the other; and that anything that I attempted to do for the members of my own race would be of no real value to them unless it was of equal value to the members of the white race by whom they were surrounded.

As this thought got hold in my mind and I began to see further into the nature of the task that I had undertaken to perform, much of the political agitation and controversy that divided the North from the South, the black man from the white, began to look unreal and artificial to me. It seemed as if the people who carried on political campaigns were engaged to a very large extent in a battle with shadows, and that these shadows represented the prejudices and animosities of a period that was now past.

On the contrary, the more I thought about it, the more it seemed to me that the kind of work that I had undertaken to do was a very real sort of thing. Moreover, it was a kind of work which tended not to divide, but to unite, all the opposing elements and forces, because it was a work of construction.

Having gone thus far, I began to consider seriously how I should proceed to gain the sympathy of each of the three groups that I have mentioned for the work that I had in hand.

I determined, first of all, that as far as possible I would try to gain the active support and cooperation in all that I undertook, of the masses of my own race. With this in view, before I began my work at Tuskegee, I spent several weeks travelling about among the rural communities of Macon County, of which Tuskegee is the county seat. During all this time I had an opportunity to meet and talk individually with a large number of people representing the rural classes, which constitute 80 per cent. of the Negro population in the South. I slept in their cabins, ate their food, talked to them in their churches, and discussed with them in their own homes their difficulties and their needs. In this way I gained a kind of knowledge which has been of great value to me in all my work since.

As years went on, I extended these visits to the adjoining counties and adjoining states. Then, as the school at Tuskegee became better known, I took advantage of the invitations that came to me to visit more distant parts of the country, where I had an opportunity to learn still more about the actual life of the people and the nature of the difficulties with which they were struggling.

In all this, my purpose was to get acquainted with the masses of the people—to gain their confidence so that I might work with them and for them.

In the course of travel and observation I became more and more impressed with the influence that the organizations which coloured people have formed among themselves exert upon the masses of the people.

The average man outside of the Negro race is likely to assume that the ten millions of coloured people in this country are a mere disorganized and heterogeneous collection of individuals, herded together under one statistical label, without head or tail, and with no conscious common purpose. This is far from true. There are certain common interests that are peculiar to all Negroes, certain channels through which it is possible to touch and influence the whole people. In my study of the race in what I may call its organized capacity, I soon learned that the most influential organization among Negroes is the Negro church. I question whether or not there is a group of ten millions of people anywhere, not excepting the Catholics, that can be so readily reached and influenced through their church organizations as the ten millions of Negroes in the United States. Of these millions of black people there is only a very small percentage that does not have formal or informal connection with some church. The principal church groups are: Baptists, African Methodists, African Methodist Episcopal Zionists, and Coloured Methodists, to which I might add about a dozen smaller denominations.

I began my work of getting the support of these organizations by speaking (or lecturing, as they are accustomed to describe it) to the coloured people in the little churches in the country surrounding the school at Tuskegee. When later I extended my journeys into other and more distant parts of the country, I began to get into touch with the leaders in the church and to learn something about the kind and extent of influence which these men exercise through the churches over the masses of the Negro people.

It has always been a great pleasure to me to meet and to talk in a plain, straightforward way with the common people of my own race wherever I have been able to meet them. But it is in the Negro churches that I have had my best opportunities for meeting and getting acquainted with them.

It has been my privilege to attend service in Trinity Church, Boston, where I heard Phillips Brooks. I have attended service in the Fifth Avenue Presbyterian Church in New York, where I heard the late Dr. John Hall. I have attended service in Westminster Abbey, in London. I have visited some of the great cathedrals in Europe when service was being held. But not any of these services have had for me the real interest that certain services among my own people have had. Let me describe the type of the service that I have enjoyed more than any other in all my experience in attending church, whether in America or Europe.

In Macon County, Ala., where I live, the coloured people have a kind of church-service that is called an "all-day meeting." The ideal season for such meetings is about the middle of May. The church-house that I have in mind is located about ten miles from town. To get the most out of the "all-day meeting" one should make an early start, say eight o'clock. During the drive one drinks in the fresh fragrance of forests and wild flowers. The church building is located near a stream of water, not far from a large, cool spring, and in the midst of a grove or primitive forest. Here the coloured people begin to come together by nine or ten o'clock in the morning. Some of them walk; most of them drive. A large number come in buggies, but many use the more primitive wagons or carts, drawn by mules, horses, or oxen. In these conveyances a whole family, from the youngest to the eldest, make the journey together. All bring baskets of food, for the "all-day meeting" is a kind of Sunday picnic or festival. Preaching, preceded by much singing, begins at about eleven o'clock. If the building is not large enough, the services are held out under the trees. Sometimes there is but one sermon; sometimes there are two or three sermons, if visiting ministers are present. The sermon over, there is more plantation singing. A collection is taken—sometimes two collections—then comes recess for dinner and recreation.

Sometimes I have seen at these "all-day meetings" as many as three thousand people present. No one goes away hungry. Large baskets, filled with the most tempting spring chicken or fresh pork, fresh vegetables, and all kinds of pies and cakes, are then opened. The people scatter in groups. Sheets or table-cloths are spread on the grass under a tree near the stream. Here old acquaintances are renewed; relatives meet members of the family whom they have not seen for months. Strangers, visitors, every one must be invited by some one else to dinner. Kneeling on the fresh grass or on broken branches of trees surrounding the food, dinner is eaten. The animals are fed and watered, and then at about three o'clock there is another sermon or two, with plenty of singing thrown in; then another collection, or perhaps two. In between these sermons I am invited to speak, and am very glad to accept the invitation. At about five o'clock the benediction is pronounced and the thousands quietly scatter to their homes with many good-bys and well-wishes. This, as I have said, is the kind of church-service that I like best. In the opportunities which I have to speak to such gatherings I feel that I have done some of my best work.

In carrying out the policy which I formed early, of making use of every opportunity to speak to the masses of the people, I have not only visited country churches and spoken at such "all-day meetings" as I have just described, but for years I have made it a practice to attend, whenever it has been possible for me to do so, every important ministers' meeting. I have also made it a practice to visit town and city churches and in this way to get acquainted with the ministers and meet the people.

During my many and long campaigns in the North, for the purpose of getting money to carry on Tuskegee Institute, it has been a great pleasure and satisfaction to me, after I have spoken in some white church or hall or at some banquet, to go directly to some coloured church for a heart-to-heart talk with my own people. The deep interest that they have shown in my work and the warmth and enthusiasm with which coloured people invariably respond to any one who talks to them frankly and sincerely in regard to matters that concern the welfare of the race, make it a pleasure to speak to them.

Many times on these trips to the North it has happened that coloured audiences have waited until ten or eleven o'clock at night for my coming. This does not mean that coloured people may not attend the other meetings which

I address, but means simply that they prefer in most cases to have me to speak to them alone. When at last I have been able to reach the church or the hall where the audience was gathered, it has been such a pleasure to meet them that I have often found myself standing on my feet until after twelve o'clock. No one thing has given me more faith in the future of the race than the fact that Negro audiences will sit for two hours or more and listen with the utmost attention to a serious discussion of any subject that has to do with their interest as a people. This is just as true of the unlettered masses as it is of the more highly educated few.

Not long ago, for example, I spoke to a large audience in the Chamber of Commerce in Cleveland, Ohio. This audience was composed for the most part of white people, and the meeting continued rather late into the night. Immediately after this meeting I was driven to the largest coloured church in Cleveland, where I found an audience of something like twenty-five hundred coloured people waiting patiently for my appearance. The church building was crowded, and many of those present, I was told, had been waiting for two or three hours.

As I entered the building an unusual scene presented itself. Each member of the audience had been provided with a little American flag, and as I appeared upon the platform, the whole audience rose to its feet and began waving these flags. The reader can, perhaps, imagine the picture of twenty-five hundred enthusiastic people each of whom is wildly waving a flag. The scene was so animated and so unexpected that it made an impression on me that I shall never forget. For an hour and a half I spoke to this audience, and, although the building was crowded until there was apparently not an inch of standing room in it, scarcely a single person left the church during this time.

Another way in which I have gained the confidence and support of the millions of my race has been in meeting the religious leaders in their various state and national gatherings. For example, every year, for a number of years past, I have been invited to deliver an address before the National Coloured Baptist Convention, which brings together four or five thousand religious leaders from all parts of the United States. In a similar way I meet, once in four years, the leaders in the various branches of the Methodist Church during their general conferences.

Invitations to address the different secret societies in their national gatherings frequently come to me also. Next to the church, I think it is safe to say that the secret societies or beneficial orders bring together greater numbers of coloured people and exercise a larger influence upon the race than any other kind of organization. One can scarcely shake hands with a coloured man without receiving some kind of grip which identifies him as a member of one or another of these many organizations.

I am reminded, in speaking of these secret societies, of an occasion at Little Rock, Ark., when, without meaning to do so, I placed my friends there in a very awkward position. It had been pretty widely advertised for some weeks before that I was to visit the city. Among the plans decided upon for my reception was a parade, in which all the secret and beneficial societies in Little Rock were to take part. Much was expected of this parade, because secret societies are numerous in Little Rock, and the occasions when they can all turn out together are rare.

A few days before I reached that city some one began to make inquiry as to which one of these orders I belonged to. When it finally became known among the rank and file that I was not a member of any of them, the committee which was preparing for the parade lost a great deal of its enthusiasm, and a sort of gloom settled down over the whole proceeding. The leading men told me that they found it quite a difficult task after that to make the people understand why they were asked to turn out to honour a person who was not a member of any of their organizations. Besides, it seemed unnatural that a Negro should not belong to some kind of order. Somehow or other, however, matters were finally straightened out; all the organizations turned out, and a most successful reception was the result.

Another agency which exercises tremendous power among Negroes is the Negro press. Few if any persons outside of the Negro race understand the power and influence of the Negro newspaper. In all, there are about two hundred newspapers published by coloured men at different points in the United States. Many of them have only a small circulation and are, therefore, having a hard struggle for existence; but they are read in their local communities. Others have built up a national circulation and are conducted with energy and intelligence. With the exception of about three, these two hundred papers have stood loyally by me in all my plans and policies to uplift the race. I have called upon them freely to aid me in making known my plans and ideas, and they have always responded in a most generous fashion to all the demands that I have made upon them.

It has been suggested to me at different times that I should purchase a Negro newspaper in order that I might have an "organ" to make known my views on matters concerning the policies and interests of the race. Certain persons have suggested also that I pay money to certain of these papers in order to make sure that they support my views.

I confess that there have frequently been times when it seemed that the easiest way to combat some statement that

I knew to be false, or to correct some impression which seemed to me peculiarly injurious, would be to have a paper of my own or to pay for the privilege of setting forth my own views in the editorial columns of some paper which I did not own.

I am convinced, however, that either of these two courses would have proved fatal. The minute it should become known—and it would be known—that I owned an "organ," the other papers would cease to support me as they now do. If I should attempt to use money with some papers, I should soon have to use it with all. If I should pay for the support of newspapers once, I should have to keep on paying all the time. Very soon I should have around me, if I should succeed in bribing them, merely a lot of hired men and no sincere and earnest supporters. Although I might gain for myself some apparent and temporary advantage in this way, I should destroy the value and influence of the very papers that support me. I say this because if I should attempt to hire men to write what they do not themselves believe, or only half believe, the articles or editorials they write would cease to have the true ring; and when they cease to have the true ring, they will exert little or no influence.

So, when I have encountered opposition or criticism in the press, I have preferred to meet it squarely. Frequently I have been able to profit by these criticisms of the newspapers. At other times, when I have felt that I was right and that those who criticised me were wrong, I have preferred to wait and let the results show. Thus, even when we differed with one another on minor points, I have usually succeeded in gaining the confidence and support of the editors of the different papers in regard to those matters and policies which seemed to me really important.

In travelling throughout the United States I have met

the Negro editors. Many of them have been to Tuskegee. It has taken me twenty years to get acquainted with them and to know them intimately. In dealing with these men I have not found it necessary to hold them at arm's-length. On the contrary, I am in the habit of speaking with them frankly and openly in regard to my plans. A number of the men who own and edit Negro newspapers are graduates or former students of the Tuskegee Institute. I go into their offices and I go to their homes. We know one another; they are my friends, and I am their friend.

In dealing with newspaper people, whether they are white or black, there is no way of getting their sympathy and support like that of actually knowing the individual men, of meeting and talking with them frequently and frankly, and of keeping them in touch with everything you do or intend to do. Money cannot purchase or control this kind of friendship.

Whenever I am in a town or city where Negro newspapers are published, I make it a point to see the editors, to go to their offices, or to invite them to visit Tuskegee. Thus we keep in close, constant, and sympathetic touch with one another. When these papers write editorials endorsing any project that I am interested in, the editors speak with authority and with intelligence because of our close personal relations. There is no more generous and helpful class of men among the Negro race in America to-day than the owners and editors of Negro newspapers.

Many times I have been asked how it is that I have secured the confidence and good wishes of so large a number of the white people of the South.

My answer in brief is that I have tried to be perfectly frank and straightforward at all times in my relations with them. Sometimes they have opposed my actions, sometimes they have not, but I have never tried to deceive them. There is no people in the world which more quickly recognizes and appreciates the qualities of frankness and sincerity, whether they are exhibited in a friend or in an opponent, in a white man or in a black man, than the white people of the South.

In my experience in dealing with men of my race I have found that there is a class that has gained a good deal of fleeting popularity for possessing what was supposed to be courage in cursing and abusing all classes of Southern white people on all possible occasions. But, as I have watched the careers of this class of Negroes, in practically every case their popularity and influence with the masses of coloured people have not been lasting. There are few races of people the masses of whom are endowed with more common-sense than the Negro, and in the long run these common people see things and men pretty much as they are.

On the other hand, there have always been in every Southern community a certain number of coloured men who have sought to gain the friendship of the white people around them in ways that were more or less dishonest. For a number of years after the close of the Civil War, for example, it was natural that practically all the Negroes should be Republicans in politics. There were, however, in nearly every community in the South, one or two coloured men who posed as Democrats. They thought that by pretending to favour the Democratic party they might make themselves popular with their white neighbours and thus gain some temporary advantage. In the majority of cases the white people saw through their pretences and did not have the respect for them that they had for the Negro who honestly voted with the party to which he felt that he belonged.

I remember hearing a prominent white Democrat remark not long ago that in the old days whenever a Negro

Democrat entered his office he always took a tight grasp upon his pocket-book. I mention these facts because I am certain that wherever I have gained the confidence of the Southern people I have done so, not by opposing them and not by truckling to them, but by acting in a straightforward manner, always seeking their good-will, but never seeking it upon false pretences.

I have made it a rule to talk *to* the Southern white people concerning what I might call their shortcomings toward the Negro rather than talk *about* them. In the last analysis, however, I have succeeded in getting the sympathy and support of so large a number of Southern white people because I have tried to recognize and to face conditions as they actually are, and have honestly tried to work with the best white people in the South to bring about a better condition.

From the first I have tried to secure the confidence and good-will of every white citizen in my own county. My experience teaches me that if a man has little or no influence with those by whose side he lives, as a rule there is something wrong with him. The best way to influence the Southern white man in your community, I have found, is to convince him that you are of value to that community. For example, if you are a teacher, the best way to get the influence of your white neighbours is to convince them that you are teaching something that will make the pupils that you educate able to do something better and more useful than they would otherwise be able to do; to show, in other words, that the education which they get adds something of value to the community.

In my own case, I have attempted from the beginning to let every white citizen in my own town see that I am as much interested in the common, every-day affairs of life as himself. I tried to let them see that the presence of Tuskegee

Institute in the community means better farms and gardens, good housekeeping, good schools, law and order. As soon as the average white man is convinced that the education of the Negro makes of him a citizen who is not always "up in the air," but one who can apply his education to the things in which every citizen is interested, much of opposition, doubt, or indifference to Negro education will disappear.

During all the years that I have lived in Macon County, Ala., I have never had the slightest trouble in either registering or casting my vote at any election. Every white person in the county knows that I am going to vote in a way that will help the county in which I live.

Many nights I have been up with the sheriff of my county, in consultation concerning law and order, seeking to assist him in getting hold of and freeing the community of criminals. More than that, Tuskegee Institute has constantly sought, directly and indirectly, to impress upon the twenty-five or thirty thousand coloured people in the surrounding county the importance of cooperating with the officers of the law in the detection and apprehension of criminals. The result is that we have one of the most orderly communities in the state. I do not believe that there is any county in the state, for example, where the prohibition laws are so strictly enforced as in Macon County, in spite of the fact that the Negroes in this county so largely outnumber the whites.

Whatever influence I have gained with the Northern white people has come about from the fact, I think, that they feel that I have tried to use their gifts honestly and in a manner to bring about real and lasting results. I learned long ago that in education as in other things nothing but honest work lasts; fraud and sham are bound to be detected in the end. I have learned, on the other hand, that if one does a good, honest job, even though it may be done in the

**THE HOUSE IN MALDEN, W.VA., IN WHICH MR. WASHINGTON LIVED
WHEN HE BEGAN TEACHING**

middle of the night when no eyes see but one's own, the results will just as surely come to light.

My experience has taught me, for example, that if there is a filthy basement or a dirty closet anywhere in the remotest part of the school grounds it will be discovered. On the other hand, if every basement or every closet—no matter how remote from the centre of the school activities—is kept clean, some one will find it and commend the care and the thoughtfulness that kept it clean.

It has always been my policy to make visitors to Tuskegee feel that they are seeing more than they expected to see. When a person has contributed, say, $20,000 for the erection of a building, I have tried to provide a larger building, a better building, than the donor expected to see. This I have found can be brought about only by keeping one's eyes constantly on all the small details. I shall never forget a remark made to me by Mr. John D. Rockefeller when I was spending an evening at his house. It was to this effect: "Always be master of the details of your work; never have too many loose outer edges or fringes."

Then, in dealing with Northern people, I have always let them know that I did not want to get away from my own race; that I was just as proud of being a Negro as they were of being white people. No one can see through a sham more quickly, whether it be in speech or in dress, than the hard-headed Northern business man.

I once knew a fine young coloured man who nearly ruined himself by pretending to be something that he was not. This young man was sent to England for several months of study. When he returned he seemed to have forgotten how to talk. He tried to ape the English accent, the English dress, the English walk. I was amused to notice sometimes, when he was off his guard, how he got his English pronunciation mixed with the ordinary American accent which he had used all of his life. So one day I quietly called him aside and said to him: "My friend, you are ruining yourself. Just drop all those frills and be yourself." I am glad to say that he had sense enough to take the advice in the right spirit, and from that time on he was a different man.

The most difficult and trying of the classes of persons with which I am brought in contact is the coloured man or woman who is ashamed of his or her colour, ashamed of his or her race and, because of this fact, is always in a bad temper. I have had opportunities, such as few coloured men have had, of meeting and getting acquainted with many of the best white people, North and South. This has never led me to desire to get away from my own people. On the contrary, I have always returned to my own people and my own work with renewed interest.

I have never at any time asked or expected that any one,

in dealing with me, should overlook or forget that I am a Negro. On the contrary, I have always recognized that, when any special honour was conferred upon me, it was conferred not in spite of my being a Negro, but because I am a Negro, and because I have persistently identified myself with every interest and with every phase of the life of my own people.

Looking back over the twenty-five and more years that have passed since that time, I realize, as I did not at that time, how the better part of my education—the education that I got after leaving school—has been in the effort to work out those problems in a way that would gain the interest and the sympathy of all three of the classes directly concerned—the Southern white man, the Northern white man, and the Negro.

In order to gain consideration from these three classes for what I was trying to do I have had to enter sympathetically into the three different points of view entertained by those three classes; I have had to consider in detail how the work that I was trying to do was going to affect the interests of all three. To do this, and at the same time continue to deal frankly and honestly with each class, has been indeed a difficult and at times a puzzling task. It has not always been easy to stick to my work and keep myself free from the distracting influences of narrow and factional points of view; but, looking back on it all after a quarter of a century, I can see that it has been worth what it cost.

III | SOME EXCEPTIONAL MEN, AND WHAT I HAVE LEARNED FROM THEM

THERE are some opportunities that come to the boy or girl who is born poor that the boy or girl who is born rich does not have. In the same way there are some advantages in belonging to a disadvantaged race. The individual or the race which has to face peculiar hardships and to overcome unusual difficulties gains an experience of men and things and gets into close and intimate touch with life in a way that is not possible to the man or woman in ordinary circumstances.

In the old slavery days, when any of the white folks were a little uncertain about the quality of a new family that had moved into the neighbourhood, they always had one last resource for determining the character and the status of the new family. When in doubt, they could always rely on old "Aunt Jenny." After "Aunt Jenny" had visited the new family and returned with her report, the question was settled. Her decision was final, because "Aunt Jenny" knew. The old-fashioned house servants gained, through their peculiar experiences, a keen sense for what was called the "quality."

In freedom also the Negro has had special opportunities

for finding out the character and the quality of the white people among whom he lives. If there is a man in the community who is habitually kind and considerate to the humblest people about him, the coloured people know about that man. On the contrary, if there is a man in that community who is unfair and unjust in his dealings with them, the coloured people know that man also.

In their own way and among themselves, the coloured people in the South still have the habit of weighing and passing judgment on the white people in their community; and, nine times out of ten, their opinion of a man is pretty accurate. A man who can always be counted on to go out of his way to assist and protect the members of an unpopular race, and who is not afraid or ashamed to show that he is interested in the efforts of the coloured people about him to improve their condition, is pretty likely to be a good citizen in other respects.

In the average Southern community, also, it is almost always the best people, those who are most highly cultured and religious, who know the coloured people best. It is the best white people who go oftenest into the Negro churches or teach in the Negro Sunday-schools. It is to individual white men of this better class that the average coloured people go most frequently for counsel and advice when they are in trouble.

The fact that I was born a Negro, and the further fact that I have all my life been engaged in a kind of work that was intended to uplift the masses of my people, has brought me in contact with many exceptional persons, both North and South. For example, it was because I was a poor boy and a Negro that I found my way to Hampton Institute, where I came under the influence of General Armstrong, who, as teacher and friend, has had a larger influence upon my life than any other person I have ever known, except my mother. As it was in my boyhood, it has been in a greater degree in my later life; because of the work I was trying to do for the Negro race I have constantly been brought into contact with men of the very highest type, generous, high-minded, enlightened, and free. As I have already suggested, a large part of my education has been gained by my personal contact with these exceptional men.

There have been times in my life when I fear that I should have lost courage to go forward if I had not had constantly before me the example of other men, some of them obscure and almost unknown outside of the communities in which they lived, whose patient, unwavering cheerfulness and good-will, in spite of difficulties, have been a continued inspiration to me.

On my way to Tuskegee for the first time I met one of the finest examples of the type of man I have tried to describe. He was a railroad conductor and his name was Capt. Isaiah C. Howard. For many years he had charge of a train on the Western Railroad of Alabama, between Montgomery and Atlanta. I do not know where Captain Howard got his education, or how much he had studied books. I do know that he was born in the South and had spent all his life there. During a period of twenty years I rarely, if ever, met a higher type of the true gentleman, North or South.

I recall one occasion in particular when I was on his train between Atlanta and Montgomery during the Christmas holiday season, when the rougher and more ignorant of my race usually travel in large numbers, and when owing to the general license that has always prevailed during the holiday season, a certain class of coloured people are likely to be more or less under the influence of whiskey.

After a time a disturbance arose in the crowd at the

lower end of the car. When Captain Howard appeared, some of the men who had been drinking spoke to him in a way that most men, white or black, would have resented. In the case of some men, the language these Negroes used might easily have furnished an occasion for a shooting, the consequences of which it was not difficult for me to picture to myself. I was deeply touched to see how, like a wise and patient father, Captain Howard handled these rough fellows. He spoke to them calmly, without the least excitement in his voice or manner, and in a few moments he had obtained almost complete order in the car. After that he gave them a few words of very sensible advice which at once won their respect and gratitude, because they understood the spirit that prompted it.

During all the time that I travelled with him I never saw Captain Howard, even under the most trying circumstances, lose his temper or grow impatient with any class of coloured people that he had to deal with. During the long trips that I used to make with him, whenever he had a little leisure time, he would drop down into the seat by my side and we would talk together, sometimes for an hour at a time, on the condition and prospects of the Negro in the South. I remember that he had very definite ideas in regard to the white man's duty and responsibility, and more than once he expressed to me his own reasons for believing that the Negro should be treated with patience and with justice. He used frequently to express the fear that, by allowing himself to get into the habit of treating Negroes with harshness, the white man in the South would be injured more than the Negro.

I have spoken of Captain Howard at some length because he represents a distinct class of white people in the South, of whom an increasing number may be found in nearly every Southern community. He possessed in a very high degree those qualities of kindness, self-control, and general good breeding which belong to the real aristocracy of the South. In his talks with me he frequently explained that he was no "professional" lover of the Negro; that, in fact, he had no special feeling for the Negro or against him, but was interested in seeing fair play for every race and every individual. He said that his real reason for wanting to give the Negro the same chance that other races have was that he loved the South, and he knew that there could be no permanent prosperity unless the lowest and poorest portion of the community was treated with the same justice as the highest and most powerful. I count it a part of my good fortune to have been thrown, early in my life in Alabama, in contact with such a man as Captain Howard. After knowing him I said to myself: "If, under the circumstances, a white man can learn to be fair to my race instead of hating it, a black man ought to be able to return the compliment."

In connection with my work in Alabama, I early made the acquaintance of another Southern white man, also an Alabamian by birth but of a different type, a man of education and high social and official standing—the late J. L. M. Curry.

It was my privilege to know Doctor Curry well during the last twenty years of his life. He had fought on the side of the Confederacy during the Civil War, he had served as a college professor and as United States Minister to Spain, and had held other high public positions. More than that, he represented, in his personal feelings and ways of thinking, all that was best in the life of the Southern white people.

Notwithstanding the high positions he had held in social and official life, Doctor Curry gave his latter years to the cause of education among the masses of white and coloured people in the South, and was never happier than when engaged in this work.

I met Doctor Curry for the first time, in a business way, at Montgomery, Ala. While I was in the Capitol building I happened to be, for a few moments, in a room adjoining that in which Doctor Curry and some other gentlemen were talking, and could not avoid overhearing their conversation. They were speaking about Negro education. One of the state officials expressed some doubt about the propriety of a Southern gentleman taking an active part in the education of the Negro. While I am not able to give his exact words, Doctor Curry replied in substance that he did not believe that he or any one else had ever lost anything, socially or in any other way, on account of his connection with Negro education.

"On the other hand," Doctor Curry continued, "I believe that Negro education has done a great deal more for me than I have ever been able to do for Negro education."

Then he went on to say that he had never visited a Negro school or performed a kindly act for a Negro man, woman, or child, that he himself was not made stronger and better for it.

Immediately after the Civil War, he said, he had been bitterly opposed to every movement that had been proposed to educate the Negro. After he came to visit some of the coloured schools, however, and saw for himself the struggles that the coloured people were making to get an education, his prejudice had changed into sympathy and admiration.

As far as my own experience goes—and I have heard the same thing said by others—there is no gentler, kindlier, or more generous type of man anywhere than those Southern white men who, born and bred to those racial and sectional differences which, after the Civil War, were mingled with and intensified by the bitterness of poverty and defeat, have struggled up to the point where they feel nothing but kindness to the people of all races and both sections. It is much easier for those who shared in the victory of the Civil War—I mean the Northern white man and the Negro—to emancipate themselves from racial and sectional narrowness.

There is another type of white man in the South who has aided me in getting a broader and more practical conception of my work. I refer to the man who has no special sentiment for or against the Negro, but appreciates the importance of the Negro race as a commercial asset—a man like Mr. John M. Parker, of New Orleans. Mr. Parker is the president of the Southern Industrial Congress, and is one of the largest planters in the Gulf states. His firm in New Orleans, I understand, buys and sells more cotton than any other firm in the world. Mr. Parker sees more clearly than any white man in the South with whom I have talked, the fact that it is important to the commercial progress of the country that the Negro should be treated with justice in the courts, in business, and in all the affairs of life. He realizes also that, in order that the Negro may have an incentive to work regularly, he must have his wants increased; and this can be brought about only through education.

I have heard many addresses to coloured people in all parts of the country, but I have never heard words more sensible, practical, and to the point from the lips of any man than those of an address which Mr. Parker delivered before nearly a thousand Negro farmers at one of the annual Negro Conferences at the Tuskegee Institute. Mr. Parker has for years been a large employer of Negro labour on his plantation. He was thus able to speak to the farmers simply and frankly, and, even though he told them some rather unpleasant truths, the audience understood and appreciated not only what was said, but the spirit in which it was uttered.

The hope of the South, so far as the interests of the

Negro are concerned, rests very largely upon men like Mr. Parker, who see the close connection between labour, industry, education, and political institutions, and have learned to face the race problem in a large and tolerant spirit, and are seeking to solve it in a practical way.

A quite different type of man with whom I have been thrown in frequent contact is Col. Henry Watterson, of the Louisville *Courier-Journal*. Colonel Watterson seems to me to represent the Southern gentleman of the old school, a man of generous impulses, high ideals, and gracious manner. I have had frequent and long conversations with him about the Negro and about conditions in the South. If there is anywhere a man who has broader or more liberal ideas concerning the Negro, or any undeveloped race, I have not met him.

A few years ago, when a meeting had been arranged at Carnegie Hall, New York, in order to interest the public in the work of our school at Tuskegee, we were disappointed in securing a distinguished speaker from the South who had promised to be present. At the last moment the committee in charge telegraphed to Colonel Watterson. Although (because of the death of one of his children) he had made up his mind not to speak again in public for some time, Colonel Watterson went to New York from Louisville and made one of the most eloquent speeches in behalf of the Negro that I have ever heard. He told me at the time that nothing but his interest in the work that we were trying to do at Tuskegee would have induced him to leave home at that time.

Whenever I have been tempted to grow embittered or discouraged about conditions in the South, my acquaintance with such men as Mr. Parker and Colonel Watterson has given me new strength and increased my faith.

I have been fortunate also in the coloured men with

whom I have been associated. There is a class of Negroes in the South who are just as much interested as the best white people in the welfare of the communities in which they live. They are just as much opposed as the best white people to anything that tends to stir up strife between the races. But there are two kinds of coloured people, just as there are two kinds of white people.

There is a class of coloured people who are narrow in their sympathies, short-sighted in their views, and bitter in their prejudices against the white people. When I first came to Alabama I had to decide whether I could unite with this class in a general crusade of denunciation against the white people of the South, in order to create sympathy in the North for the work that I was seeking to carry on, or whether I would consider the real interests of the masses of my race, and seek to preserve and promote the good relations that already existed between the races.

I do not deny that I was frequently tempted, during the early years of my work, to join in the general denunciation of the evils and injustice that I saw about me. But when I thought the matter over, I saw that such a course would accomplish no good and that it would do a great deal of harm. For one thing, it would serve only to mislead the masses of my own race in regard to the opportunities that existed right about them. Besides that, I saw that the masses of the Negro people had no disposition to carry on any general war against the white people. What they wanted was the help and encouragement of their white neighbours in their efforts to get an education and to improve themselves.

Among the coloured men who saw all this quite as clearly as myself was Rufus Herron, of Camp Hill, Ala. He was born in slavery and had had almost no school advantages, but he was not lacking in practical wisdom and he was a leader in the community in which he lived. Some years ago, after he had harvested his cotton crop he called to see me at the Tuskegee Institute. He said that he had sold all of his cotton, had got a good price for it, had paid all his debts for the year, and had twenty dollars remaining. He handed me ten dollars and asked me to use it in the education of a student at Tuskegee. He returned to his home and gave the other ten to the teacher of the white school in his vicinity, and asked him to use it in the education of a white student.

Since that day I have come to know Rufus Herron well. He never misses a session of the annual Tuskegee Negro conference. He is the kind of man that one likes to listen to because he always says something that goes straight to the point, and after he has covered the subject he stops. I do not think that I have ever talked with him that he did not have something to suggest in regard to the material, educational, and moral improvement of the people, or something that might promote better relations between white people and black people. If there is a white man, North or South, that has more love for his community or his country than Rufus Herron, it has not been my good fortune to meet him. In his feelings and ambitions he also is what I have called an aristocrat.

I have no disposition to deny to any one, black or white, the privilege of speaking out and protesting against wrong and injustice, whenever and wherever they choose to do so. I would do injustice to the facts and to the masses of my people in the South, however, if I did not point out how much more useful a man like Rufus Herron has made his life than the man who spends his time and makes a profession of going about talking about his "rights" and stirring up bitterness between the white people and coloured people. The salvation of the Negro race in America is to be worked out, for the most part, not by abstract argument and not by mere denunciation of wrong, but by actual achievement in constructive work.

In Nashville there is another coloured man—a banker, a man of education, wealth, and culture. James C. Napier is about the same age as Rufus Herron. I have been closely associated with him for twenty years. I have been with him in the North and in the South; I have worked with him in conventions, and I have talked with him in private in my home and in his home. During all the years that I have known him I have never heard Mr. Napier express a narrow or bitter thought toward the white race. On the contrary, he has shown himself anxious to give publicity to the best deeds of the white people rather than the worst. During the greater part of my life I have done my work in association with such men as he. There is no part of the United States in which I have not met some of this type of coloured men. I honour such men all the more because, had they chosen to do so, they could easily have made themselves and those about them continually miserable by dwelling upon the mean things which people say about the race or the injustices which are so often a part of the life of the Negro.

Let me add that, so far as I have been able to see, there is no real reason why a Negro in this country should make himself miserable or unhappy. The average white man in the United States has the idea that the average Negro spends most of his time in bemoaning the fact that he is not a white man, or in trying to devise some way by which he will be permitted to mingle, in a purely social way, with white people. This is far from the truth. In my intercourse with all classes of the Negro, North and South, it is a rare occurrence when the matter of getting away from the race, or of social intermingling with the white people, is so much as mentioned. It is especially true that intelligent Negroes find a satisfaction in social intercourse among themselves that is rarely known or understood by any one outside of the Negro race. In their family life, in the secret societies and churches, as well as other organizations where coloured people come together, the most absorbing topic of conversation invariably relates to some enterprise for the betterment of the race.

Among coloured farmers, as among white farmers, the main topic of discussion is naturally the farm. The Negro is, in my opinion, naturally a farmer, and he is at his very best when he is in close contact with the soil. There is something in the atmosphere of the farm that develops and strengthens the Negro's natural common-sense. As a rule the Negro farmer has a rare gift of getting at the sense of things and of stating in picturesque language what he has learned. The explanation of it is, it seems to me, that the Negro farmer studies nature. In his own way he studies the soil, the development of plants and animals, the streams, the birds, and the changes of the seasons. He has a chance of getting the kind of knowledge that is valuable to him at firsthand.

In a visit some years ago to a Negro farmers' institute in the country, I got a lesson from an unlettered coloured farmer which I have never forgotten. I had been invited by one of the Tuskegee graduates to go into the country some miles from Tuskegee to be present at this institute. When I entered the room the members of the institute were holding what they called their farmers' experience meeting. One coloured farmer was asked to come up to the platform and give his experience. He was an old man, about sixty-five years of age. He had had no education in the book, but the teacher had reached him, as he had others in the community, and showed him how to improve his methods of farming.

When this old man came up to the front of the room to tell his experience, he said: "I'se never had no chance to study no science, but since dis teacher has been here I'se been trying to make some science for myself."

Thereupon he laid upon the table by his side six stalks of cotton and began to describe in detail how, during the last ten years, he had gradually enriched his land so as to increase the number of bolls of cotton grown upon each individual stalk. He picked up one stalk and showed it to the audience; before the teacher came to the community, he said, and before he began to improve his land, his cotton produced only two bolls to the stalk. The second year he reached the point where, on the same land, he succeeded in producing four bolls on a stalk. Then he showed the second stalk to the audience. After that he picked up the third and fourth stalks, saying that during the last few years he had reached a point where a stalk produced eight bolls.

Finally he picked up the last stalk and said:

"This year I made cotton like dis"—and he showed a stalk containing fourteen bolls. Then the old fellow took his seat.

Some one in the audience from a distance arose and said: "Uncle, will you tell us your name?"

The old fellow arose and said: "Now, as you ask me for my name, I'll tell you. In de old days, before dis teacher come here, I lived in a little log-cabin on rented land, and had to mortgage my crop every year for food. When I didn't have nothin', in dem days, in my community dey used to call me 'Old Jim Hill.' But now I'se out o' debt; I'se de deeds for fifty acres of land; and I lives in a nice house wid four rooms that's painted inside and outside; I'se got some money in de bank; I'se a taxpayer in my community; I'se edicated my children. And now, in my community, dey calls me 'Mr. James Hill.'"

The old fellow had not only learned to raise cotton during these ten years, but, so far as he was concerned, he had solved the race problem.

As one travels through the Southland, he is continually meeting old Negro farmers like the one that I have described. It has been one of the great satisfactions of my life to be able from time to time to go out into the heart of the country, on the plantations and on the farms where the masses of the coloured people live. I like to get into the fields and into the woods where they are at work and talk with them. I like to attend their churches and Sunday-schools and camp-meetings and revival meetings. In this way I have gotten more material which has been of service to me in writing and speaking than I have ever gotten by reading books. There are no frills about the ordinary Negro farmer, no pretence. He, at least, is himself and no one else. There is no type of man that I more enjoy meeting and knowing.

A disadvantaged race has, too, the advantage of coming in contact with the best in the North, and this again has been my good fortune. There are two classes of people in the North—one that is just as narrow and unreasonable toward the white man at the South as any Southern white man can be toward the Negro or a Northern white man. I have always chosen to deal with the other white man at the North—the man with large and liberal views.

In saying this I make an exception of the "professional" friend of the Negro. I have little patience with the man who parades himself as the "professional" friend of any race. The "professional" friend of the Chinese or Japanese or Filipino is frequently a well-meaning person, but he is always tiresome. I like to meet the man who is interested in the Negro because he is a human being. I like to talk with the man who wants to help the Negro because he is a member of the human family, and because he believes that, in helping the Negro, he is helping to make this a better world to live in.

During the twenty-five years and more that I have been accustomed to go North every year to obtain funds with which to build up and support the Tuskegee Institute, I have made the acquaintance of a large number of exceptional people in that part of the country. Because I was seeking aid for Negro education, seeking assistance in giving opportunities to a neglected portion of our population, I had an opportunity to meet these people in a different and, perhaps, more intimate way than the average man. I had an opportunity to see a side of their lives of which many of their business acquaintances, perhaps, did not know the existence.

Few people, I dare say, who were acquainted with the late Mr. H. H. Rogers, former head of the Standard Oil Company, knew that he had any special interest or sympathy for the Negro. I remember well, however, an occasion when he showed this interest and sympathy. I was showing him one day the copy of a little Negro farmers' newspaper, published at Tuskegee, containing an account of the efforts the people in one of our country communities were making to raise a sum of money among themselves in order that they might receive the aid he had promised them in building a school house. As Mr. Rogers read the account of this school "rally," as it was called, and looked down the long list of names of the individuals who in order to make up the required sum, had contributed out of their poverty, some a penny, some five cents, some twenty-five, some a dollar and a few as much as five dollars, his eyes filled with tears. I do not think he ever before realized, as he did at that moment, the great power—and the great power for good—which his money gave them.

During the last years of his life, Mr. Rogers was greatly

interested in the building of the Virginian Railway, which was constructed upon his own plans and almost wholly with his own capital, from Norfolk, Va., to Deep Water, W. Va. One of the first things he did, after this new railway was completed, was to make arrangements for a special train in order that I might travel over and speak at the different towns to the coloured people along the line and, at the same time, study their situation in order that something might be done to improve their condition. From his point of view, these people were part of the resources of the country which he wanted to develop. He desired to see the whole country through which this railway passed, which, up to that time, had remained in a somewhat backward condition, made prosperous and flourishing and filled with thriving towns and with an industrious and happy people. He died, however, just as he seemed on the eve of realizing this dream.

For a number of years before his death, I knew Mr. H. H. Rogers intimately. I used to see him frequently in his office in New York; sometimes I made trips with him on his yacht. At such times I had opportunity to talk over in detail the work that I was trying to do. Mr. Rogers had one of the most powerful and resourceful minds of any man I ever met. His connection with large business affairs had given him a broad vision and practical grasp of public and social questions, and I learned much from my contact with him.

In this connection I might name another individual who represents another and entirely different type of man, with whom I have frequently come in contact during my travels through the Northern states. I refer to Mr. Oswald Garrison Villard, editor of the New York *Evening Post*. Mr. Villard is not primarily a business man in the sense that Mr. Rogers was, and his interest in the education and progress of the Negro is of a very different kind from that of Mr.

Rogers; at least he approaches the matter from a very different point of view.

Mr. Villard is the grandson of William Lloyd Garrison, the abolitionist. He is a literary man and idealist, and he cherishes all the intense zeal for the rights of the Negro which his grandfather before him displayed. He is anxious and determined that the Negro shall have every right and every opportunity that any other race of people has in this country. He is the outspoken opponent of every institution and every individual who seeks to limit in any way the freedom of any man or class of men anywhere. He has not only continued in the same way and by much the same methods that his grandfather used, to fight the battles for human liberty, but he has interested himself in the education of the Negro. It is due to the suggestion and largely to the work of Mr. Villard that Tuskegee, at the celebration of its twenty-fifth anniversary received the $150,000 memorial fund to commemorate the name and service of Mr. William H. Baldwin to Tuskegee and Negro education in the South. Mr. Villard has given much of his time and personal service to the work of helping and building up some of the smaller and struggling Negro schools in the South. He is a trustee of at least two of such institutions, being president of the board of trustees in one case, and takes an active part in the direction and control of their work. He has recently been active and, in fact, is largely responsible for the organization of the National Association for the Advancement of the Coloured People, a sort of national vigilance committee, which will watch over and guard the rights and interests of the race, and seek through the courts, through legislation, and through other public and private means, to redress the wrongs from which the race now suffers in different parts of the country.

Perhaps I ought to add in fairness that, while I sympathize fully with Mr. Villard's purposes, I have frequently differed with him as to the methods he has used to accomplish them. Sometimes he has criticised me publicly in his newspaper and privately in conversation. Nevertheless, during all this time, I have always felt that I retained his friendship and good-will. I do not think there has ever been a time when I went to him with a request of any kind either for myself personally or to obtain his help in any way in the work in which I was engaged that he has not shown himself willing and anxious to do everything in his power to assist me. While I have not always been able to follow his suggestions, or agree with him as to the methods I should pursue, I have, nevertheless, I think, profited by his criticism and have always felt and appreciated the bracing effect upon public sentiment of his vigorous and uncompromising spirit.

I have learned also from Mr. Villard the lesson that persons who have a common purpose may still maintain helpful, friendly relations, even if they do differ as to details and choose to travel to the common goal by different roads.

Another man who has exercised a deep influence upon me is Robert C. Ogden. Some months after I became a student at Hampton Institute, Mr. Robert C. Ogden, in company with a number of other gentlemen from New York, came to Hampton on a visit. It was the first time I ever saw him and the first sight of a man of the physical, mental, and moral build of Mr. Ogden—strong, fresh, clean, vigorous—made an impression upon me that it is hard for any one not in my situation to appreciate. The thing that impressed me most was this: Here was a man, intensely earnest and practical, a man who was deeply engrossed in business affairs, who still found time to turn aside from his business and give a portion of his time and thought to the elevation of an unfortunate race.

Mr. Ogden is a man of a very different type from either Mr. Rogers or Mr. Villard. He does not look at the question of uplifting the Negro as a question of rights and liberty exclusively: he does not think of it merely as a means of developing one of the neglected resources of the South. He looks upon it, if I may venture to say so, as a question of humanity. Mr. Ogden is intensely interested in human beings; he cannot think of an unfortunate individual or class of individuals without feeling a strong impulse to help them. He has spent a large portion of his time, energy, and fortune in inspiring a large number of other people with that same sentiment. I do not believe any man has done more than Mr. Odgen to spread, among the masses of the people, a spirit of unselfish service to the interests of humanity, irrespective of geographical, sectarian or racial distinction.

Perhaps I can in no better way give an idea of what Mr. Ogden has accomplished in this direction than by giving a list of some of the activities in which he has been engaged. Mr. Ogden is:

President and only Northern member of the Conference for Southern Education,

President of the Southern Education Board,

President of the Board of Trustees of Hampton Institute,

Trustee of Tuskegee Institute,

Trustee of the Anna T. Jeans Fund for Improvement of the Negro Common School,

Member of the General Education Board.

From this it will be seen that Mr. Ogden is directly connected with almost every important movement for education in the South, whether for white people or for black people. In addition to that he is president of the Board of Directors of the Union Theological Seminary of New York, member of the Sage Foundation Board, and of the Presbyterian Board of Home Missions. In all these different directions he has worked quietly, steadily, without stinting himself, for the good of the whole country. Many of the sentiments which he has expressed in his annual addresses at the meetings of these different organizations have in them the breadth of view of a real statesman. His idea was that in giving an equal opportunity for education to every class in the community he was laying the foundation for a real democracy. He spoke of the educational conference, for instance, as "a congress called by the voice of 'democracy'"; and again he said of this same institution, "Its foundation is the proposition that every American child is entitled to an education."

In spite of what he has done in a multitude of ways to advance education, I have heard Mr. Ogden say, both in public and in private, that he was not an educated man. Perhaps he has not gotten so much education in the usual, formal, technical matter out of books as some other people. But through the study of books, or men, or things, Mr. Ogden has secured the finest kind of education, and deserves to be classed with the scholars of the world. So far as I have studied Mr. Ogden's career, it is of interest and value to the public in three directions:

First: He has been a successful business man.

Second: More than any other one individual except Gen. S. C. Armstrong, he has been the leader in a movement to educate the whole South, regardless of race or colour.

Third: In many important matters relating to moral and religious education in the North, Mr. Ogden is an important leader.

I know of few men in America whose life can be held up before young people as a model as can Mr. Ogden's life.

It would be difficult for me to describe or define the manner and extent to which I have been influenced and educated by my contact with Mr. Ogden. It was characteristic of him, that the only reason I came to know him is because I needed him, needed him in the work which I was trying to do. Had I not been a Negro I would probably never have had the rare experience of meeting and knowing intimately a man who stands so high in every walk of life as Mr. Robert C. Ogden. Had Mr. Ogden been a weak man, seeking his own peace of mind and social position, he would not have been brave enough and strong enough to ignore adverse criticism in his efforts to serve the unfortunate of both races in the South, and in that case I should probably not have made his acquaintance.

The men that I have mentioned are but types of many others, men intellectually and spiritually great, who, directly and indirectly, have given comfort, help, and counsel to the ten millions of my race in America.

IV | MY EXPERIENCE WITH REPORTERS AND NEWSPAPERS

I HAVE learned much from reporters and newspapers. Seldom do I go into any city, or even step out on the platform between trains, but that it seems to me some newspaper reporter finds me. I used to be surprised at the unexpected places in which these representatives of the press would turn up, and still more surprised and sometimes embarrassed by the questions they would ask me. It seemed to me that, if there was any particular thing that I happened to know and did not feel at liberty to talk about, that would be the precise thing that the reporter who met me wanted to question me about. In such cases, too, the reporter usually got the information he wanted, or, if he didn't, I was sorry afterward, because if the actual facts had been published they would have done less damage than the half truths which he did get hold of.

I confess that when I was less experienced I used to dread reporters. For a long time I used to look upon a reporter as a kind of professional pry, a sort of social mischief-maker, who was constantly trying to find out something that would make trouble. The consequence was that when I met reporters I was likely to find myself laying plans to circumvent them and keep them in the dark in regard to my purposes and business.

A wide acquaintance with newspapers and newspaper men has completely changed my attitude toward them. In the first place I have discovered that reporters usually ask just the questions that the average man in the community in which the newspapers are located would ask if he had the courage to do so. The only difference is that the reporter comes out squarely and plumply and asks you the question that another person would ask indirectly of some one else.

For my part, I have found it both interesting and important to know what sort of questions the average man in the community was asking, for example about the progress of the Negro, or about my work. The sort of questions the reporters in the different parts of the country ask indicate pretty clearly, not only what the people in the community know about my work, but they tell me a great deal, also, about the feeling of the average man toward the members of my race in that community and toward the Negro generally. Not only do the newspaper reporters keep me informed, in the way I have described, in regard to a great many things I want to know, but frequently, by the questions that they ask, they enable me to correct false impressions and to give information which it seems important the public should have, in regard to the condition and progress of the Negro.

One other consideration has changed my attitude toward the reporters. As I have become better acquainted with newspapers I have come to understand the manner and extent to which they represent the interests and habits of thought of the people who read and support them. Any man who is engaged in any sort of work that makes constant demands upon the good-will and confidence of the public knows that it is important that he should have an opportunity to reach this public directly and to answer just the sort of questions the newspapers ask of him. As I have said, these inquiries represent the natural inquiries of the average man. If the newspaper did not ask and answer these questions, they would remain unanswered, or the public would get the information it wanted from some more indirect and less reliable source.

Several times, during the years that I have been at Tuskegee, a representative from some Southern paper or magazine has come to me to inquire in regard to some rumour or report that has got abroad in regard to conditions inside our school. In such cases I have simply told the reporter to take as much time as he chose and make as thorough an examination of the school and everything about it as he cared to. At the same time, I have assured him that he was perfectly free to ask any questions on any subject, of any person that he met on the grounds. In other words, I have given him every opportunity to go as far as he wanted, and to make his investigation as thorough as he desired.

Of course, in every institution as large as ours, there is abundant opportunity for a malicious or ill-disposed person to make injurious criticism, or to interpret what he learns in a way that would injure the institution. But in every such case, instead of printing anything derogatory to the school, the newspaper investigation has proved the most valuable sort of advertisement, and the rumours that had been floating about have been silenced. There is no means so effectual in putting an end to gossip as a newspaper investigation and report. On the other hand, I have found that there is no way of so quickly securing the good-will of a newspaper reporter as by showing him that you have nothing to conceal.

Frequently I have heard people criticise the newspapers because they print and give currency to so much that is merely trivial; in other words, what we commonly speak of as gossip. What I know of the newspapers convinces me that they do not print one tenth of the reports that are sent in to them, and that a large part of the time of every newspaper man is spent in running down and proving the falsity of stories and rumours that have gained currency in the community as a result of the natural disposition of mankind to accept and believe any kind of statement that is sufficiently circumstantial and interesting. My own experience leads me to believe that if the newspaper performed no other service for the community but that of rooting out of the public mind the malice and prejudice that rest upon misinformation and gossip, it would justify its existence in this way alone.

In saying this, I do not overlook the fact that daily papers are responsible for giving currency to many statements that are false and misleading: that too frequently the emphasis is placed upon the things that are merely exciting, while important matters—or, at least, matters that seem important to some of us who are on the outside—are passed over in silence. To a very large extent the daily newspapers have merely taken up the work that was formerly performed by the village gossip, or by the men who sat around in the village store, talked politics, and made public opinion. The newspaper, however, does that work on a higher plane. It gives us a world-wide outlook, and it makes a commendable effort to get the truth. Even if, like the village gossip, it puts the emphasis sometimes on the wrong things and spends a lot of time over personal and unimportant matters, it at least brings all classes of people together in doing so. People who read the same newspaper are bound to feel neighbourly, even though they may never meet one another, even though they live thousands of miles apart.

I have learned much from newspapers and from newspaper men. I think I have met all kinds of newspaper reporters, not only those who work on the conservative, but also those on the so-called "yellow" journals, and what I have seen of them convinces me that no class of men in the community work harder or more faithfully to perform the difficult tasks to which they are assigned or, considering all the circumstances, perform their work better. I confess that I have grown to the point where I always like to meet and talk with newspaper men, because they know the world, they know what is going on, and they know men. I have frequently been amazed, in talking with newspaper men, to learn the amount of accurate, intimate, and inside information that they had about public and even private matters, and at the insight they showed in weighing and judging public men and their actions.

One thing that has interested me in this connection has been the discovery that practically every large newspaper in the country has in its office a vast array of facts which, out of charity for the individuals concerned or because some public interest would be injured by their publication, never get into print. I am convinced that much more frequently than is supposed newspaper men show their interest in individuals and in the public welfare by what they withhold from publication rather than by what they actually do print. Considering that, under the conditions in which modern newspapers are conducted, any fact which would interest and excite the community has become a kind of commodity which it is the business of the newspaper to gather up and sell, it is surprising that these publications are as discriminating and as considerate as they are.

It seems to me, also, that there has been a noticeable improvement, in recent years, in the method of getting and preparing newspaper reports. I am not sure whether this is due more to the improvement in the class of men who represent the papers or whether it is due to a better understanding on the part of the public as to the methods of dealing with reporters; to a more definite recognition on the part of both the public and the newspapers of the responsible position which the modern newspaper occupies in the complex organization of modern social life. Both private individuals and public men seem to have recognized the fact that, in a country where the life of every individual touches so closely the life of every other, it is in the interest of all that each should work, as it were, in the open, where all the world may know and understand what he is doing.

On the other hand, newspapers have discovered that the only justification for putting any fact in a newspaper is that publication will serve some sort of public interest, and that, in the long run, the value of a piece of news and the reputation of a newspaper that prints it depend upon the absolute accuracy and trustworthiness of its reports.

I have learned something about newspapers and newspaper men from my own experience with them, but I have learned much, also, from the manner in which some of the best known men in this country have been accustomed to deal with them.

On several occasions when I was at the White House, during the time that Colonel Roosevelt was President, I saw him surrounded by half a dozen reporters—representing great daily papers. I was greatly surprised on those occasions to observe that the President would talk to these reporters just as frankly and freely about matters pertaining to the government, and his plans and policies, as one partner in business would talk to another partner. While these men, as a result of the interview, would telegraph long despatches to their papers, I am sure I am safe in saying that the President's confidence was rarely, if ever, betrayed.

It was largely through such frank interviews, taking the whole country into his confidence, as it were, that President Roosevelt was able, in so large a degree, to carry the whole country along with him. Ever since I have known Colonel Roosevelt, one of the things that I have observed in his career has been his ability and disposition to keep in close personal touch with the brightest newspaper men and magazine writers of the country. The newspaper men like him because he understands the conditions under which they work and at the same time recognizes the important part that they and their reports play in the actual, if not in the official, government in a democratic country like ours.

Another noted man whom it has been my privilege to see a good deal of, in connection with newspapers, is Mr. Andrew Carnegie. Not long ago I heard the question asked why it was that, while so many rich men were unpopular, Andrew Carnegie held the love and respect of the common people. From what I have seen of Mr. Carnegie I ascribe a good deal of his popularity to the candour and good sense with which he deals with reporters and newspapers. Mr. Carnegie has something of Mr. Roosevelt's disposition to take reporters into his confidence. Both Colonel Roosevelt and Mr. Carnegie have known how to use newspapers as a means of letting the world know what they are doing and, in both cases, I believe that the popularity of these men is due, in very large part, to their ability to get into a sort of personal touch with the masses of the people through the newspapers.

In saying this I do not mean that either Colonel Roo-

sevelt or Mr. Carnegie has made use of the newspapers
merely for the sake of increasing their personal popularity.
The man who is known, and has the confidence of the
public, can, if he does not allow himself to be fooled by his
own popularity, accomplish a great deal more, perform a
much greater public service, than the man whose name is
unknown.

In the case of both Colonel Roosevelt and Mr. Carnegie,
the names of private individuals have, in each case, become
associated in the public mind with certain large public interests. They have come to be, in a very real sense, public men
because they have embodied in their persons and their lives
certain important public interests. Although, so far as I know,
he has never held public office of any kind, Mr. Carnegie is
nevertheless a public man. Mr. Roosevelt has not ceased to
be identified with certain important public interests; nor has
he lost, to any great extent, political power because he is no
longer President of the United States. The power which
these men exercise upon the minds and hearts of the masses
of their fellow countrymen is largely due to the fact that they
were able to make the acquaintance of the public through
the newspapers.

I have always counted it a great privilege that my name
became associated, comparatively early in my life, with what
has always seemed to me a great and important public
interest, namely, a form of education which seems to me
best suited to fit a recently enfranchised race for the duties
and responsibilities of citizenship in a republic. The fact that
I have been compelled to raise the larger part of the money
for establishing this kind of education by direct appeals to
the public has made my name pretty generally known. I am
glad that this is true, for through the medium of the newspapers I have been able to get in touch with many hundreds

and thousands of persons that I would never have been able to reach with my voice. All this has multiplied my powers for service a hundredfold.

Of course it is just as true that a man who has become well known and gained the confidence of the public through the medium of the press can use that power for purely selfish purposes, if he chooses, as that he can use it for the public welfare. I have no doubt that nearly every man who has in any way gained the confidence of the public has every year many opportunities for turning his popularity to private account.

Several times in the course of a year, for example, some one makes me a present of shares of stock in some new concern, and, on several occasions, I have had deeds of lots in some land scheme or new town presented to me. I have made it a rule to promptly return every gift of that kind, first of all for the good business reason that it would not pay me to have my name connected with any enterprise, no matter how legitimate it might be, for which I could not be personally responsible, and the use of my name, under such circumstances, so far as it influenced any one to invest in the scheme, would be a fraud.

A second reason is my desire to keep faith with the public, if I may so express it. In order to do that, I have never been able to see how I could afford to give any of my time or attention to any enterprise or any kind of work that did not have to do specifically and directly with the work of Negro education, in the broad spirit in which I have interpreted it.

I have already said that, in my early experience with newspaper reporters, I used to think it was necessary to be very careful in letting them know what my ambitions and aims in regard to my work were. But I have learned that it is pretty hard to keep anything from the newspapers that the newspapers think the public wants to know. As a result of what I have learned I try to be perfectly frank with news-paper men. For some years I have made it my custom to talk with them concerning all my plans and everything of a public nature in which I am interested. I talk with them just the same as I would with one of my friends or business acquaintances. When a reporter comes to interview me I tell him what I wish he might publish, and what I wish he would not publish. Frequently I have discovered that the newspaper man understood better than I how to state things in a way that should give the right impression to the public. This seems to be especially true of the Washington corre-spondents of the great dailies, who, considering the many important matters which they have to handle, exercise, it seems to me, a remarkable discretion as to what should, and should not, be printed.

Let me give an illustration: When Colonel Roosevelt was President, he invited me to come to the White House to read over an important part of one of his annual messages to Congress. The passage of his message in regard to which he consulted me referred to a subject upon which there was great interest at that time, and the newspaper reporters in Washington, and especially those on duty at the White House, had some inkling as to the subject that the President wished to discuss with me. I was with the President for a considerable time. When I came out of the President's office I was at once surrounded by half a dozen newspaper men who wished me to tell them, in detail, just what I had dis-cussed with the President. After some hesitation I made up my mind to try the experiment of being perfectly frank with them. I gave them an outline of what was in the mes-sage and went into some detail in regard to our discussion of it. After I had given them the facts, I said to them: "Now, gentlemen, do you think that this is a subject that I ought to give out to the public at this time through the newspapers?"

Each one of them promptly replied that he did not think it was a matter that I ought to give out to the public. The result was that the next day not a single newspaper represented in this conversation had a line concerning the matter which had called me to the White House. This is an example of an experience which I have frequently had in dealing with reporters. If I had tried to hide something from them, or to deceive them, I suspect that some garbled report or misstatement of the facts would have been given to the public in regard to the matter.

There is always a question with me, and I presume there is with most public speakers, as to what is the best form of preparing and delivering a public address, and of getting the gist of it correctly and properly reported through the newspapers. When I first began speaking in public I used to follow the plan to a great extent of committing speeches to memory. This plan, however, I soon gave up. At present I do not commit speeches to memory, except on very important occasions, or when I am to speak on an entirely new subject.

The plan of writing out one's speech and reading it has its advantages, but it also has its disadvantages. A written speech is apt to sound stiff and formal; besides, if one depends upon a manuscript, he will not be able to adapt himself to the occasion. Writing out a speech, however, has the advantage of enabling one to give out something to the newspapers that will be absolutely accurate.

After trying both the plan of committing to memory and of writing out my addresses, I have struck upon a compromise which I find, in my case, answers the purpose pretty well. The plan which I now follow is this: I think out what

I want to say pretty carefully. After having done that, I write head lines, or little suggestions that will call my attention to the points that I wish to make in covering my speech. After having thought out the general line of my speech, and then having prepared my head lines, I have for a number of years been accustomed to dictate my speech to a stenographer. By long practice, I have found that, after dictating my speech, I can take my head lines or memorandum sheet and follow the dictation almost exactly when I deliver my address. I give out all or a portion of the dictated address to the newspapers in advance. This the reporters consider an accommodation to them. It insures accuracy and at the same time leaves me free while speaking to throw aside the stiffness and formality that would naturally be necessary in reading an address or in delivering an address that had been committed to memory, and to take advantage of any local interests that would give a more lively colour to what I have to say.

Another disadvantage of a written address, or of one committed to memory, is that it is difficult to adapt it to the interests of the immediate audience. To me, talking to an audience is like talking to an individual. Each audience has a personality of its own, and one can no more find two audiences that are exactly alike than he can find two individuals that are exactly alike. The speaker who fails to adapt himself to the conditions, surroundings, and general atmosphere of his audience in a large degree fails, I think, as a speaker. I have found that the best plan is, as I have stated, to study one's subject through and through, to saturate himself with it so that he is master of every detail, and then use head lines as a memorandum.

One of the questions which I suppose, every man who deals with the public has to meet sooner or later is how to deal with a false newspaper report. I have made it a rule never to deny a false report, except under very exceptional circumstances. In nine cases out of ten the denying of the report simply calls attention to the original statement in a way to magnify it. Many people who did not see the original false report will see the denial and will then begin to search for the original report to find out what it was. And then, unfortunately, there are always some newspapers that will spread a report that is not justified by facts, for the purpose of securing a denial or of exciting a discussion. My experience is that it always gives a certain dignity and standing to a slander or a falsehood to deny it. Every one likes a fight, and a controversy will frequently lend a fictitious interest and importance to comparatively trivial circumstances.

During a long period of years in dealing with the public I have been deceived only once in recent years by a newspaper reporter. This was the case of a man on a New York paper who got aboard a train with me, took a seat by my side, and began the discussion of a question which was much before the public at that time. He gave me the impression that he was a man engaged in business and was only incidentally interested in the subject under discussion. I talked with him pretty freely and frankly, as I would with any gentleman. My suspicions were not aroused until I noticed that suddenly and unceremoniously he left the train at a way station. I at once made up my mind that I had been talking, not to an individual but to the public. The next morning a long report of this interview appeared in his paper. I at once informed the managing editor of what had occurred.

I am not sure that anything definite came of my letter, but I believe that one way to improve the methods of the newspapers in dealing with individuals is to protest when you think you have been badly treated.

The important thing, it seems to me, about the newspaper is that it represents the interest and reflects the opinions and intelligence of the average man in the community where the paper is published. The local press reflects the local prejudice. Its failings are the common human failings. Its faults are the faults of the average man in the community, and on the whole it seems to me best that it should be so. If the newspapers were not a reflex of the minds of their readers, they would not be as interesting or as valuable as they are. We should not know the people about us as well as we do. As long as the newspaper exists we not only have a means of understanding how the average man thinks and feels, but we have a medium for reaching and influencing him. People who profess to have no respect for the newspapers as a rule, I fear, have very little understanding or respect for the average man.

The real trouble with the newspapers is that while they frequently exhibit the average man at his worst, they rarely show him at his best. In order to read the best about the average man we must still go to books or to magazines. The newspaper has the advantage that it touches real things and real persons, but it touches them only on the surface. For that reason I have found it safe never to give too much weight to what a newspaper says about a man either good or bad.

Nevertheless I have learned more from newspapers than I have from books. In fact, aside from what I have learned from actual contact with men and with things, I believe I have gained the greatest part of my education from newspapers. I am sure this is so if I include among the newspapers those magazines which deal with current topics. Certainly I have been stimulated in all my thinking more by news than I have by the general statements I have met in books. In this, as in other matters, I like to deal at first-hand with the raw material and this I find in the newspapers more than in books.

Frequently I have heard persons speak of the newspaper as if its only purpose in making its reports was to tear down rather than build up. It is certainly true that newspapers are rather ruthless in the way in which they seem to bring every man, particularly every public man, to the bar of public opinion and make him explain and justify his work.

Nevertheless it is important that every man who is in any way engaged, directly or indirectly, in performing any kind of public service should never be permitted to forget that the only title to place or privilege that any man enjoys in the community is ultimately based on the service that he performs. I believe that any man, public or private, who meets newspaper men and deals with the newspaper in that spirit will find himself helped immensely in his work by the press rather than injured.

For my own part I feel sure that I owe much of such success as I have been able to achieve to the sympathy and interest which the newspaper press, North and South, has shown in the work that I have been trying to do. Largely through the medium of the newspapers I have been able to come into contact with the larger public outside of my community and the circle of my immediate friends and, by this means, to make the school at Tuskegee, not merely a private philanthropy, but in the truest sense of that word a public institution, supported by the public and conducted not in the interest of any one race or section, merely, but in the interest of the whole country.

THE INTELLECTUALS AND THE BOSTON MOB

V

I T MAKES a great deal of difference in the life of a race, as it does in the life of an individual, whether the world expects much or little of that individual or of that race. I suppose that every boy and every girl born in poverty have felt at some time in their lives the weight of the world against them. What the people in the communities did not expect them to do it was hard for them to convince themselves that they could do.

After I got so that I could read a little, I used to take a great deal of satisfaction in the lives of men who had risen by their own efforts from poverty to success. It is a great thing for a boy to be able to read books of that kind. It not only inspires him with the desire to do something and make something of his life, but it teaches him that success depends upon his ability to do something useful, to perform some kind of service that the world wants.

The trouble in my case, as in that of other coloured boys of any age, was that the stories we read in school were all concerned with the success and achievements of white boys and men. Occasionally I spoke to some of my schoolmates in regard to the characters of whom I had read, but they invariably reminded me that the stories I had been reading had to do with the members of another race. Sometimes I tried to argue the matter with them, saying that what others had done some of us might also be able to do, and that the lack of a past in our race was no reason why it should not have a future.

They replied that our case was entirely different. They said, in effect, that because of our colour and because we carried in our faces the brand of a race that had been in slavery, white people did not want us to succeed.

In the end I usually wound up the discussion by recalling the life of Frederick Douglass, reminding them of the high position which he had reached and of the great service which he had performed for his own race and for the cause of human freedom in the long anti-slavery struggle.

Even before I had learned to read books or newspapers, I remember hearing my mother and other coloured people in our part of the country speak about Frederick Douglass's wonderful life and achievements. I heard so much about Douglass when I was a boy that one of the reasons why I wanted to go to school and learn to read was that I might read for myself what he had written and said. In fact, one of the first books that I remember reading was his own story of his life, which Mr. Douglass published under the title of "My Life and Times." This book made a deep impression upon me, and I read it many times.

After I became a student at Hampton, under Gen. Samuel C. Armstrong, I heard a great deal more about Frederick Douglass, and I followed all his movements with intense interest. At the same time I began to learn something about other prominent and successful coloured men who were at that time the leaders of my race in the United States.

HON. P. B. S. PINCHBACK OF LOUISIANA

Lieutenant-Governor 1871–72,
and afterward Congressman

These were such men as Congressman John M. Langston, of Virginia; United States Senator Blanche K. Bruce, of Mississippi; Lieut.-Gov. P. B. S. Pinchback, of Louisiana; Congressman John R. Lynch, of Mississippi; and others whose names were household words among the masses of the coloured people at that time. I read with the greatest eagerness everything I could get hold of regarding the prominent Negro characters of that period, and was a faithful student of their lives and deeds. Later on I had the privilege of meeting and knowing all of these men, but at that time I little thought that it would ever be my fortune to meet and know any of them.

On one occasion, when I happened to be in Washington, I heard that Frederick Douglass was going to make a speech in a near-by town. I had never seen him nor heard him speak, so I took advantage of the opportu-

BLANCHE K. BRUCE OF MISSISSIPPI

Who was born a slave, but was the first Negro to become a member of the United States Senate

MAJOR JOHN R. LYNCH, U.S.A.

Who served as a member of Congress
from Mississippi

nity. I was profoundly impressed both by the man and by the address, but I did not dare approach even to shake hands with him. Some three or four years after I had organized the Tuskegee Institute I invited Mr. Douglass to make a visit to the school and to speak at the commencement exercises of the school. He came and spoke to a great audience, many of whom had driven thirty or forty miles to hear the great orator and leader of the race. In the course of time I invited all of the prominent coloured men whose names I have mentioned, as well as others, to come to Tuskegee and speak to our students and to the coloured people in our community.

As a matter of course, the speeches (as well as the writings) of most of these men were concerned for the most part with the past history, or with the present and future political prob-

CHARLES BANKS

"He has taught me the value of common-sense
in dealing with conditions as they exist
in the South"

lems, of the Negro race. Mr. Douglass's great life-work had been in the political agitation that led to the destruction of slavery. He had been the great defender of the race, and in the struggle to win from Congress and from the country at large the recognition of the Negro's rights as a man and a citizen he had played an important part. But the long and bitter political struggle in which he had engaged against slavery had not prepared Mr. Douglass to take up the equally difficult task of fitting the Negro for the opportunities and responsibilities of freedom. The same was true to a large extent of other Negro leaders. At the time when I met these men and heard them speak I was invariably impressed, though young and inexperienced, that there was something lacking in their public utterances. I felt that the millions of Negroes needed something more than to be reminded of their sufferings and of their political rights; that they needed to do something more than merely to defend themselves.

Frederick Douglass died in February, 1895. In September of the same year I delivered an address in Atlanta at the Cotton States Exposition.

I spoke in Atlanta to an audience composed of leading Southern white people, Northern white people, and members of my own race. This seemed to me to be the time and the place, without condemning what had been done, to emphasize what ought to be done. I felt that we needed a policy, not of destruction, but of construction; not of defence, but of aggression; a policy, not of hostility or surrender, but of friendship and advance. I stated, as vigorously as I was able, that usefulness in the community where we resided was our surest and most potent protection.

One other point which I made plain in this speech was that, in my opinion, the Negro should seek constantly in every manly, straightforward manner to make friends of the white man by whose side he lived, rather than to content himself with seeking the good-will of some man a thousand miles away.

While I was fully convinced, in my own mind, that the policy which I had outlined was the correct one, I was not at all prepared for the widespread interest with which my words were received.

I received telegrams and congratulations from all parts of the country and from many persons whose names I did not know or had heard of only indirectly through the newspapers or otherwise. Very soon invitations began to come to me in large numbers to speak before all kinds of bodies and on all kinds of subjects. In many cases I was offered for my addresses what appeared to me almost fabulous sums. Some of the lecture bureaus offered me as high as $300 and $400 a night for as long a period as I would speak for them. Among other things which came to me was an offer from a prominent Western newspaper of $1000 and all expenses for my services if I would describe for it a famous prize-fight.

I was invited, here and there, to take part in political campaigns, especially in states where the Negro vote was important. Lecture bureaus not only urged upon me the acceptance of their offers through letters, but even sent agents to Tuskegee. Newspapers and magazines made generous offers to me to write special articles for them. I decided, however, to wait until I could get my bearings. Apparently the words which I had spoken at Atlanta, simple and almost commonplace as they were, had touched a deep and responsive chord in the public mind.* This gave me

---

*The following is copied from the official history of the exposition:

"Then came Booker T. Washington, who was destined to make a national reputation in the next fifteen minutes. He appeared on the programme by invitation of the directors as the representative of the Negro race. This would appear to have been a natural arrangement, if not a matter of course, and it seems strange flow that there should

much to think about. In the meantime I determined to stick close to my work at Tuskegee.

One of the most surprising results of my Atlanta speech was the number of letters, telegrams, and newspaper editorials that came pouring in upon me from all parts of the country, demanding that I take the place of "leader of the Negro people," left vacant by Frederick Douglass's death, or assuming that I had already taken this place. Until these suggestions began to pour in upon me, I never had the remotest idea that I should be selected or looked upon, in any such sense as Frederick Douglass had been, as a leader of the Negro people. I was at that time merely a Negro school teacher in a rather obscure industrial school. I had devoted all my time and attention to the work of organizing and bringing into existence the Tuskegee Institute, and I did not know just what the functions and duties of a leader were, or what was expected of him on the part of the coloured people or of the rest of the world. It was not long, however, before I began to find out what was expected of me in the new position into which a sudden newspaper notoriety seemed to have thrust me.

---

have been any doubt as to the wisdom or propriety of giving the Negro a place in the opening exercises. Nevertheless, there was, and the question was carefully, even anxiously, considered before was decided. There were apprehensions that the matter would encourage social equality and prove offensive to the white people, and in the end unsatisfactory to the coloured race. But the discussion satisfied the board that this course was right, and they resolved to risk the expediency of doing right. The sequel showed the wisdom of their decision. The orator himself touched upon the subject with great tact, and the recognition that was given has greatly tended to promote good feeling between the races, while the wide and self-respecting course of the Negroes on that occasion has raised them greatly in the estimation of their white fellow-citizens."

In introducing the speaker, Governor Bullock said: "We have with us to-day the representative of Negro enterprise and Negro civilization. I have the honour to introduce to you Prof. Booker T. Washington, principal of the Tuskegee Normal and Industrial College, who will formally present the Negro exhibit."

Professor Washington was greeted with applause, and his speech received marked attention.

I was not a little embarrassed, when I first began to appear in public, to find myself continually referred to as "the successor of Frederick Douglass." Wherever I spoke—whether in the North or in the South—I found, thanks to the advertising I had received, that large audiences turned out to hear me.

It has been interesting, and sometimes amusing, to note the amount and variety of disinterested advice received by a man whose name is to any extent before the public. During the time that my Atlanta address was, so to speak, under discussion, and almost every day since, I have received one or more letters advising me and directing my course in regard to matters of public interest.

One day I receive a letter, or my attention is called to some newspaper editorial, in which I am advised to stick to my work at Tuskegee and put aside every other interest that I may have in the advancement of my race. A day or two later I may receive a letter, or read an editorial in a newspaper, saying that I am making a mistake in confining my attention entirely to Tuskegee, to Negro education, or even to the Negro in the United States. It has been frequently urged upon me, for example, that I ought, in some way or other, to extend the work that we are trying to do at Tuskegee to Africa or to the West Indies, where Negroes are a larger part of the population than in this country.

There has been a small number of white people and an equally small number of coloured people who felt, after my Atlanta speech, that I ought to branch out and discuss political questions, putting emphasis upon the importance of political activity and success for the members of my race. Others, who thought it quite natural that, while I was in the South, I should not say anything that would be offensive, expected that I would cut loose in the North and denounce the Southern people in a way to keep alive and intensify the sectional differences which had sprung up as a result of slavery and the Civil War. Still others thought that there was something lacking in my style of defending the Negro. I went too much into the facts and did not say enough about the Rights of Man and the Declaration of Independence.

When these people found that I did not change my policy as a result of my Atlanta speech, but stuck to my old line of argument, urging the importance of education of the hand, the head, and the heart, they were thoroughly disappointed. So far as my addresses made it appear that the race troubles in the South could be solved by education rather than by political measures, they felt that I was putting the emphasis in the wrong place.

I confess that all these criticisms and suggestions were not without effect upon my mind. But, after thinking the matter all over, I decided that, pleasant as it might be to follow the programme that was laid out for me, I should be compelled to stick to my original job and work out my salvation along the lines that I had originally laid down for myself.

My determination to stand by the programme which I had worked out during the years that I had been at Tuskegee and which I had expressed in my Atlanta speech, soon brought me into conflict with a small group of coloured people who sometimes styled themselves "The Intellectuals," at other times "The Talented Tenth." As most of these men were graduates of Northern colleges and made their homes for the most part in the North, it was natural enough, I suppose, that they should feel that leadership in all race matters should remain, as heretofore, in the North. At any rate, they were opposed to any change from the policy of uncompromising and relentless antagonism to the South so long as there seemed to them to be anything in Southern conditions wrong or unjust to the Negro.

My life in the South and years of study and effort in connection with actual and concrete problems of Southern life had given me a different notion, and I believed that I had gained some knowledge and some insight which they were not able to obtain in the same degree at a distance and from the study of books.

The first thing to which they objected was my plan for the industrial education of the Negro. It seemed to them that in teaching coloured people to work with the hands I was making too great a concession to public opinion in the South. Some of them thought, probably, that I did not really believe in industrial education myself; but in any case they were opposed to any "concession," no matter whether industrial education was good or bad.

According to their way of looking at the matter, the Southern white man was the natural enemy of the Negro, and any attempt, no matter for what purpose, to gain his sympathy or support must be regarded as a kind of treason to the race.

All these matters furnished fruitful subjects for controversy, in all of which the college graduates that I have referred to were naturally the leaders. The first thing that such a young man was tempted to do after leaving college was, it seems, to start out on a lecturing tour, travelling about from one town to another for the purpose of discussing what are known as "race" subjects.

I remember one young man in particular who graduated from Yale University and afterward took a post-graduate course at Harvard, and who began his career by delivering a series of lectures on "The Mistakes of Booker T. Washington." It was not long, however, before he found that he could not live continuously on my mistakes. Then he discovered that in all his long schooling he had not fitted himself to perform any kind of useful and productive labour. After he had failed in several other directions he appealed to me, and I tried to find something for him to do. It is pretty hard, however, to help a young man who has started wrong. Once he gets the idea that—because he has crammed his head full with mere book knowledge—the world owes him a living, it is hard for him to change. The last I heard of the young man in question, he was trying to eke out a miserable existence as a book agent while he was looking about for a position somewhere with the Government as a janitor or for some other equally humble occupation.

When I meet cases, as I frequently do, of such unfortunate and misguided young men as I have described, I cannot but feel the most profound sympathy for them, because I know that they are not wholly to blame for their condition. I know that, in nine cases out of ten, they have gained the idea at some point in their career that, because they are Negroes, they are entitled to the special sympathy of the world, and they have thus got into the habit of relying on this sympathy rather than on their own efforts to make their way.

In college they gave little thought or attention to preparing for any definite task in the world, but started out with the idea of preparing themselves to solve the race problem. They learned in college a great deal about the history of New England freedom; their minds were filled with the traditions of the anti-slavery struggle; and they came out of college with the idea that the only thing necessary to solve at once every problem in the South was to apply the principles of the Declaration of Independence and the Bill of Rights. They had learned in their studies little of the actual present-day conditions in the South and had not considered the profound difference between the political problem and the educational problem, between the work of destruction and of construction, as it applies to the task of race building.

Among the most trying class of people with whom I come in contact are the persons who have been educated in books to the extent that they are able, upon every occasion, to quote a phrase or a sentiment from Shakespeare, Milton, Cicero, or some other great writer. Every time any problem arises they are on the spot with a phrase or a quotation. No problem is so difficult that they are not able, with a definition or abstraction of some kind, to solve it. I like phrases, and I frequently find them useful and convenient in conversation, but I have not found in them a solution for many of the actual problems of life.

In college they studied problems and solved them on paper. But these problems had already been solved by some one else, and all that they had to do was to learn the answers. They had never faced any unsolved problems in college, and all that they had learned had not taught them the patience and persistence which alone solve real problems.

I remember hearing this fact illustrated in a very apt way by a coloured minister some years ago. After great sacrifice and effort he had constructed in the South a building to be used for the purpose of sheltering orphans and aged coloured women. After this minister had succeeded in getting his building constructed and paid for, a young coloured man came to inspect it and at once began pointing out the defects in the building. The minister listened patiently for some time and then, turning to the young man, he said: "My friend, you have an advantage over me." Then he paused and looked at the young man, and the young man looked inquiringly at the minister, who continued: "I am not able to find fault with any building which you have constructed."

Perhaps I ought to add, in order that my statements may not be misleading, that I do not mean to say that the type of college man that I have described is confined to the members of my own race. Every kind of life produces its own peculiar kind of failures, and they are not confined to one race. It would be quite as wrong for me to give the impression that the description which I have given applies to all coloured graduates of New England or other colleges and to none others. As a matter of fact, almost from the beginning we have had men from these colleges at Tuskegee; I have come into contact with others at work in various institutions of the South; and I have found that some of the sanest and most useful workers were those who had graduated at Harvard and other New England colleges. Those to whom I have referred are the exception rather than the rule.

There is another class of coloured people who make a business of keeping the troubles, the wrongs, and the hardships of the Negro race before the public. Having learned that they are able to make a living out of their troubles, they have grown into the settled habit of advertising their wrongs— partly because they want sympathy and partly because it pays. Some of these people do not want the Negro to lose his grievances, because they do not want to lose their jobs.

A story told me by a coloured man in South Carolina will illustrate how people sometimes get into situations where they do not like to part with their grievances. In a certain community there was a coloured doctor of the old school, who knew little about modern ideas of medicine, but who in some way had gained the confidence of the people and had made considerable money by his own peculiar methods of treatment. In this community there was an old lady who happened to be pretty well provided with this world's goods and who thought that she had a cancer. For twenty years she had enjoyed the luxury of having this old doctor treat her for that cancer. As the old doctor became— thanks to the cancer and to other practice—pretty well-to-do, he decided to send one of his boys to a medical college. After graduating from the medical school, the young man returned home, and his father took a vacation. During this time the old lady who was afflicted with the "cancer" called in the young man, who treated her; within a few weeks the cancer (or what was supposed to be the cancer) disappeared, and the old lady declared herself well.

When the father of the boy returned and found the patient on her feet and perfectly well, he was outraged. He called the young man before him and said: "My son, I find that you have cured that cancer case of mine. Now, son, let me tell you something. I educated you on that cancer. I put you through high school, through college, and finally through the medical school on that cancer. And now you, with your new ideas of practising medicine, have come here and cured that cancer. Let me tell you, son, you have started all wrong. How do you expect to make a living practising medicine in that way?"

I am afraid that there is a certain class of race-problem solvers who don't want the patient to get well, because as long as the disease holds out they have not only an easy means of making a living, but also an easy medium through which to make themselves prominent before the public.

My experience is that people who call themselves "The Intellectuals" understand theories, but they do not understand things. I have long been convinced that, if these men could have gone into the South and taken up and become interested in some practical work which would have brought them in touch with people and things, the whole world would have looked very different to them. Bad as conditions might have seemed at first, when they saw that actual progress was being made, they would have taken a more hopeful view of the situation.

But the environment in which they were raised had cast them in another world. For them there was nothing to do but insist on the application of the abstract principles of protest. Indignation meetings in Faneuil Hall, Boston, became at one time so frequent as to be a nuisance. It would not have been so bad if the meetings had been confined to the subjects for which they were proposed; but when "The Intellectuals" found that the Southern people rarely, if ever, heard of their protests and, if they did hear of them, paid no attention to them, they began to attack the persons nearer home. They began to attack the people of Boston because they said that the people of Boston had lost interest in the cause of the Negro. After attacking the friends of the Negro elsewhere, particularly all those who happened to disagree with them as to the exact method of aiding the Negro, they made me a frequent and favourite object of attack—not merely for the reasons which I have already stated, but because they felt that if they attacked me in some particularly violent way it would surprise people and attract attention. There is no satisfaction in holding meetings and formulating protests unless you can get them into the newspapers. I do not really believe that these people think as badly of the person whom they have attacked at different times as their words would indicate. They are merely using them as a sort of sounding-board or megaphone to make their own voices carry farther. The persistence and success with which these men sought this kind of advertising has led the general public to believe the number of my opponents among the Negro masses to be much larger than it actually is.

A few years ago when I was in Boston and the subject of

those who were opposing me was under discussion, a coloured friend of mine, who did not belong to the so-called "Talented Tenth," used an illustration which has stuck in my mind. He was originally from the South, although he had lived in Boston for a number of years. He said that he had once lived in Virginia, near a fashionable hotel. One day a bright idea struck him and he went to the proprietor of the hotel and made a bargain to furnish him regularly with a large number of frogs, which were in great demand as a table delicacy. The proprietor asked him how many he could furnish. My friend replied that he felt quite sure that he could furnish him with a cartload, if necessary, once a week. The bargain was concluded. The man was to deliver at the hotel the following day as large a number of frogs as possible.

When he appeared, my friend had just six frogs. The proprietor looked at the frogs, and then at my friend.

"Where are the others?" he said.

"Well, it is this way," my friend replied; "for months I had heard those bull-frogs in a pond near my house, and they made so much noise that I supposed there were at least a million of them there. When I came to investigate, however, I found that there were only six."

Inspired by their ambition to "make themselves heard," and, as they said, compel the public to pay attention to their grievances, this little group kept up their agitation in various forms and at different places, until their plans culminated one night in Boston in 1903. To convince the public how deep and sincere they were in their peculiar views, and how profoundly opposed they were to every one who had a different opinion, they determined to do something desperate. The coloured citizens of Boston had asked me to deliver an address before them in one of their largest churches. The meeting was widely advertised, and there was a large audience present. Unknown to any of my coloured friends in Boston, this group, who, as I have stated, were mostly graduates of New England colleges, organized a mob to disturb the meeting and to break it up if possible. The presiding officer at the meeting was the Hon. William H. Lewis, a graduate of Amherst College and of the Harvard Law School. Various members of the group were scattered in different parts of the church. In addition to themselves there were present in the audience—and this, better than anything else, shows how far they had been carried in their fanaticism—some of the lowest men and women from vile dens in Boston, whom they had in some way or other induced to come in and help them disturb the meeting.

As soon as I began speaking, the leaders, stationed in various parts of the house, began asking questions. In this and in a number of other ways they tried to make it impossible for me to speak. Naturally the rest of the audience resented this, and eventually it was necessary to call in the police and arrest the disturbers.

Of course, as soon as the disturbance was over, most of those who had participated in it were ashamed of what they had done. Many of those who had classed themselves with "The Intellectuals" before, hastened to disavow any sympathy with the methods of the men who had organized the disturbance. Many who had before been lukewarm in their friendship became my closest friends. Of course the two leaders, who were afterward convicted and compelled to serve a sentence in the Charles Street Jail, remained unrepentant. They tried to convince themselves that they had been made martyrs in a great cause, but they did not get much encouragement in this notion from other coloured people, because it was not possible for them to make clear just what the cause was for which they had suffered.

The masses of coloured people in Boston and in the United States indorsed me by resolution and condemned the disturbers of the meeting. The Negro newspapers as a whole were scathing in their criticism of them. For weeks afterward my mail was filled with letters from coloured people, asking me to visit various sections and speak to the people.

I was intensely interested in observing the results of this disturbance. For one thing I wanted to find out whether a principle in human nature that I had frequently observed elsewhere would prove true in this case.

I have found in my dealings with the Negro race—and I believe that the same is true of all races—that the only way to hold people together is by means of a constructive, progressive programme. It is not argument, nor criticism, nor hatred, but work in constructive effort, that gets hold of men and binds them together in a way to make them rally to the support of a common cause.

Before many weeks had passed, these leaders began to disagree among themselves. Then they began to quarrel, and one by one they began to drop away. The result is that, at the present time, the group has been almost completely dispersed and scattered. Many of "The Intellectuals" today do not speak to one another.

The most surprising thing about this disturbance, I confess, is the fact that it was organized by the very people who have been loudest in condemning the Southern white people because they had suppressed the expression of opinion on public questions and denied the Negro the right of free speech.

As a matter of fact, I have talked to audiences in every part of this country; I have talked to coloured audiences in the North and to white audiences in the South; I have talked to audiences of both races in all parts of the South;

A type of the unpretentious cabin which an Alabama Negro formerly occupied
and the modern home in which he now lives

everywhere I have spoken frankly and, I believe, sincerely on
everything that I had in my mind and heart to say. When I
had something to say about the white people I said it to the

white people; when I had something to say about coloured people I said it to coloured people. In all these years—that is the curious thing about it—no effort has been made, so far as I can remember, to interrupt or to break up a meeting at which I was present until it was attempted by "The Intellectuals" of my own race in Boston.

I have gone to some length to describe this incident because it seems to me to show clearly the defects of that type of mind which the so-called "Intellectuals" of the race represent.

I do not wish to give the impression by what I have said that, behind all the intemperance and extravagance of these men, there is not a vein of genuine feeling and even at times of something like real heroism. The trouble is that all this fervour and intensity is wasted on side issues and trivial matters. It does not connect itself with anything that is helpful and constructive. These crusaders, as nearly as I can see, are fighting windmills.

The truth is, I suspect, as I have already suggested, that "The Intellectuals" live too much in the past. They know books but they do not know men. They know a great deal about the slavery controversy, for example, but they know almost nothing about the Negro. Especially are they ignorant in regard to the actual needs of the masses of the coloured people in the South to-day.

There are some things that one individual can do for another, and there are some things that one race can do for another. But, on the whole, every individual and every race must work out its own salvation. Let me add that if one thing more than another has taught me to have confidence in the masses of my own people it has been their willingness (and even eagerness) to learn and their disposition to help themselves and depend upon themselves as soon as they have learned how to do so.

VI | A COMMENCEMENT ORATION ON CABBAGES

O NE of the advantages of a new people or a new race—such as, to a very large extent, the American Negroes are—consists in the fact that they are not hampered, as other peoples sometimes are, by tradition. In the matter of education, for example, Negroes in the South are not hampered by tradition, because they have never had any worth speaking of. As a race we are free, if we so choose, to adopt at once the very latest and most approved methods of education, because we are not held back by any wornout tradition; and we have few bad educational habits to be got rid of before we can start in to employ newer and better methods.

I have sometimes regarded it as a fortunate circumstance that I never studied pedagogy. If I had done so, every time I attempted to do anything in a new way I should have felt compelled to reckon with all the past, and in my case that would have taken so much time that I should never have got anywhere. As it was, I was perfectly free to go ahead and do whatever seemed necessary at the time, without reference to whether that same thing had ever been done by any one else at any previous time or not.

As an illustration of the way in which too much learning will hamper a man who finds himself in the presence of
a new problem—one not in the books—I recall the fate of
the young Harvard graduate who was a teacher at Tuskegee
for one or two sessions several years ago. This young man
had very little practical experience as a teacher, but he had
made a special study of the subject of education while he
was in college; largely because of his high scholarship, he was
given a position as teacher of education at Tuskegee.

I am afraid that, until he arrived, we knew very little
about pedagogy at Tuskegee. He proceeded to enlighten us,
however. He lectured and preached to us about Comenius,
Rousseau, Pestalozzi, and all the others, and what he said
was very interesting. The trouble was that he made a complete failure in his own classes. But that was not all. We were
trying to fit our students to go out as teachers in the rural
districts. I pointed out to him that if he were going to help
them to any great extent it would be necessary for him to
study the conditions of the country people and to get
acquainted with some of the actual problems of a small, rural
Negro community. He did not seem to regard that as
important, because, as he said, the principles were the same
in every case and all that was necessary was to apply them.

I told him, then, that I thought we had worked out at
Tuskegee a number of definite methods of dealing with the
problems of these rural communities, and suggested to him
that if he wanted to teach the general principles he ought to
work out a theory for these methods, so that the teachers
and students might understand the principles under which
they were actually working. He did not seem to take this
suggestion seriously. It seemed absurd to him that any one
should come down to the Black Belt of Alabama to look for
anything new in the matter of education. In short, his mind

was so burdened with the traditions and knowledge of other systems of education that he could not see anything in any kind of education that seemed to break with these traditions. In fact, he seemed to feel, whenever he did discover anything new or strange about the methods that we employed, that there must be something either wrong or dangerous about them.

My own early experience was, I suppose, like that of most other teachers; I picked up quite naturally those methods of teaching that were in vogue around me or that seemed to be prescribed by the textbooks. My method consisted in asking pupils to learn what was in the book, and then requiring them to recite it.

I shall long remember the time when the folly and uselessness of much of the old-time method of teaching first fairly dawned upon me. I was teaching a country school near my old home in West Virginia. This school was located near a piece of land that was wet and marshy, but nevertheless beautiful in appearance. It was June and the day was hot and sultry; when the usual recess or playtime came, I was as anxious as the children were to get outside of the close and stuffy school room into the open air. That day I prolonged the playtime to more than twice the usual period.

The hour previous to recess had been employed by me in trying to get a class of children interested in what proved to be a rather stupid geography lesson. I had been asking my pupils a lot of dull and tiresome questions, getting them to define and name lakes, capes, peninsulas, islands, and so forth. Naturally the answers of the children were quite as dull and stupid as the questions.

As soon as the children were out of doors at playtime, however, they all, as if by common instinct, scampered off into the marshes. In a few seconds they were wading in the cool water, jumping about in the fragrant grass, and enjoying themselves in a way that was in striking contrast to the dull labour of the geography lesson. I soon became infected with the general fever; and in a few minutes I found myself following the children at a rapid rate and entering into the full enjoyment of the contrast between the dull, dead atmosphere of the school room and the vivid tingling sense of the living out-doors.

We had not been out of the school house and away from the old geography lesson long before one of the boys who had been among the dullest in his recitation in the school room became the leader of a sort of exploring party. Under his leadership we began to discover, as we waded along the stream, dozens of islands, capes, and peninsulas, with here and there a little lake or bay, which, as some of the pupils pointed out, would furnish a safe harbour for ships if the stream were only large enough. Soon every one of the children was busy pointing out and naming the natural divisions of land and water. And then, after a few days, we got pieces of wood and bark and let them float down the stream; we imagined them to be great ships carrying their cargoes of merchandise from one part of the world to another. We studied the way the stream wandered about in the level land, and noticed how the little sand bars and the corresponding harbours were formed by the particles of sand and earth which were rolled down by the stream. We located cities on these harbours, and tried to find water-power where we might build up manufacturing centres.

Before long I discovered that, quite unconsciously, we had taken up again the lessons in the school room and were studying geography after a new fashion. This time, however, we found a real joy and zest in the work, and I think both teacher and pupils learned more geography in that short period than they ever learned in the same space of time before or since.

For the first time the real difference between studying about things through the medium of books, and studying things themselves without the medium of books, was revealed to me. The children in this recess period had gained more ideas in regard to the natural divisions of the earth than they would have gained in several days by merely studying geography inside the school room. To be sure, they had not learned the names, the locations, nor the definitions of the capes, bays, and islands, but they had learned what was more important—to *think* capes, islands, and peninsulas. From that time on they found no difficulty and were really greatly interested in recognizing the natural divisions of land and water wherever they met them.

The lesson that I learned thus early in my experience as a teacher I have never forgotten. In all my work at Tuskegee Institute I have lost no opportunity to impress upon our teachers the importance of training their students to study, analyze, and compare actual things, and to use what they have learned in the school room and in the text-book, to enable them to observe, think about, and deal with the objects and situations of actual life.

Not long ago I visited the class room of a new teacher at Tuskegee, who was conducting a class in measurements. This teacher had insisted that each member of the class should commit to memory the tables of measurement, and when I came in they were engaged in reciting, singsong, something that sounded like a sort of litany composed of feet, yards, rods, acres, gills, pints, quarts, ounces, pounds, and the rest. I looked on at this proceeding for a few minutes; then a happy thought occurred to me and I asked the teacher to let me take the class in hand. I began by asking if anyone in the class had ever measured the class room in which they were sitting. There was a dumb silence. Then I asked if any one had ever marked off an acre of actual land, had ever measured a gill of water, or had ever weighed an ounce or a pound of sugar. Not a hand was raised in reply.

Then I told the teacher that I would like to take charge of the class for a few days. Before the week was over I had seen to it that every member of the class had supplied himself with a rule or a measure of some sort. Under my direction the students measured the class room and found what it would cost to paint the walls of the room.

From the class room we went to a part of the farm where the students were engaged in planting sweet potatoes. Soon we had an acre of sweet potatoes measured off. We computed the number of bushels raised on that acre and calculated the cost and profit of raising them.

Before the week was over the whole class had been through the boarding department, where they had an opportunity to weigh actual sugar. From the steward we obtained some interesting figures as to how much sugar was used a day; then we computed how much was used by each student. We went to the farm again and weighed a live pig, and I had the class find out the selling price of pork on that particular day, not in Chicago, but in Alabama. I had them calculate the amount that—not an imaginary pig or a pig in Chicago—the pig that they had weighed would bring that day in the local market. It took some time to go through all these operations, but I think that it paid to do so. Besides, it was fun. It was fun for me, and it was a great deal more fun for the students. Incidentally the teacher got an awakening and learned a lesson that I dare say he has never forgotten.

At the present time all teachers in the academic studies are expected to make a careful study of the work carried on

Ordinarily, at the closing exercises of a high school, [grad]uates are expected to stand up on the platform and, out [of a]ll their inexperience, instruct their elders how to suc[cee]d in life. We were fortunate at Tuskegee, in the thirty-[seve]n industries carried on there and in the thousand acres [of l]and that are cultivated, to be able to give our students, in [add]ition to their general education, a pretty good knowl[edg]e of some one of the familiar trades or vocations. They [hav]e, therefore, something to talk about in their essays in [wh]ich all of the audience are interested and with which all [are] more or less familiar.

Instead of having a boy or girl read a paper on some [sub]ject like "Beyond the Alps Lies Italy," we have them [exp]lain and demonstrate to the audience how to build a [roo]f, or the proper way to make cheese, or how to hatch [chi]ckens with an incubator. Perhaps one of the graduates in [the] nurses' training school will show how to lend "first aid [to t]he injured." If a girl is taking the course in dairying, she [wil]l not only describe what she has learned but will go [thro]ugh, on the platform, the various methods of operating [a m]odern dairy.

Instead of letting a boy tell why one ought to do right, [we] ask him to tell what he has learned about the feeding of [pig]s, about their diseases, and the care of them when they [are] sick. In such a case the student will have the pig on the [pla]tform, in order to illustrate the methods of caring for it, [and] demonstrate to the audience the points that he is trying [to] make.

One of our students, in his commencement oration last [Ma]y, gave a description of how he planted and raised an acre [of c]abbages. Piled high upon the platform by his side were [som]e of the largest and finest cabbages that I have ever seen. [He] told how and where he had obtained the seed; he

by the students in the industries. Nearly every day, for example, some class in mathematics, goes under the charge of a teacher, into the shops or the dairy or out on the farm to get its problems in mathematics at first hand. Students are sent from the English classes to look up the history of some trade, or some single operation performed by students in the shop, and to write out an account of that trade or that operation for the benefit of the other members of the class. In such cases attention is paid not merely to the form in which the report is written, but more especially to the accuracy and clearness of the statement. The student who prepares that kind of paper is writing something in which other students have a practical interest, and if students are not accurate there are always one or more students in the class who know enough about the subject to criticise and correct the statements made. The student in this case finds himself dealing with live matters, and he naturally feels responsibility for the statements that he makes—a responsibility that he would not feel if he were merely putting together facts that he had gathered from some encyclopædia or other second-hand source of information.

In emphasizing the importance of studying things rather than books, I do not mean to underrate the importance of studying history, general literature, or any of the other so-called cultural studies. I do think, however, that it is important that young men and young women should first of all get clear and definite ideas of things right about them, because these are the ideas by which they are going to measure and interpret things farther removed from their practical interests. To young, inexperienced minds there seems to be a kind of fatal charm about the vague, the distant, and the mysterious.

In the early days of freedom, when education was a new

thing, the boy who went away to school had a very natural human ambition to be able to come back home in order to delight and astonish the old folks with the new and strange things that he had learned. If he could speak a few words in some strange tongue that his parents had never heard before, or read a few sentences out of a book with strange and mysterious characters, he was able to make them very proud and happy. There was a constant temptation therefore for schools and teachers to keep everything connected with education in a sort of twilight realm of the mysterious and supernatural. Quite unconsciously they created in the minds of their pupils the impression that a boy or a girl who had passed through certain educational forms and ceremonies had been initiated into some sort of secret knowledge that was inaccessible to the rest of the world. Connected with this was the notion that because a man had passed through these educational forms and ceremonies he had somehow become a sort of superior being set apart from the rest of the world—a member of the "Talented Tenth" or some other ill-defined and exclusive caste.

Nothing, in my opinion, could be more fatal to the success of a student or to the cause of education than the general acceptance of any such ideas. In the long run it will be found that neither black people nor white people want such an education for their children, and they will not support schools that give it.

My experience has taught me that the surest way to success in education, and in any other line for that matter, is to stick close to the common and familiar things—things that concern the greater part of the people the greater part of the time.

I want to see education as common as grass, and as free for all as sunshine and rain.

The way to open opportunities of e... one, however, is to teach things that ev... know. I venture to say that anything in a... with the object of fitting students to p... food, for example, will win approval and... school. The reason is simple: every hum... ested, several times a day, in the subject of... part of the world is interested, either direct... its production and sale.

Not long ago I attended the closing e... school in a community composed mainly... humble walks of life. The general theme... addresses was "An Imaginary Trip to Europ... audience was bored, and I was not surpris... of people went to sleep. As a matter of fac... that the parents of a single student who... these addresses had ever been to Europe... opportunity to go at any time in the near f... did not touch a common chord. It was t... from all the practical, human interests of wh... experience. The average family in America... engaged in travelling through Europe for a... the time. Besides that, none of the member... ating class had ever been to Europe; consequ... not writing about something of which th... knowledge.

Some years ago, in an effort to bring ou... commencement exercises into a little closer... things, we tried the experiment at Tuskegee... dents write papers on some subject of which... hand knowledge. As a matter of fact, I believe... was the first institution that attempted to r... mencement exercises in this particular direct...

described his method of preparing and enriching the soil, of working the land, and harvesting the crop; and he summed up by giving the cost of the whole operation. In the course of his account of this comparatively simple operation, this student had made use of much that he had learned in composition, grammar, mathematics, chemistry, and agriculture. He had not merely woven into his narrative all these various elements that I have referred to, but he had given the audience (which was made up largely of coloured farmers from the surrounding country) some useful and practical information in regard to a subject which they understood and were interested in. I wish that any one who does not believe it possible to make a subject like cabbages interesting in a commencement oration could have heard the hearty cheers which greeted the speaker when, at the close of his speech, he held up one of the largest cabbages on the platform for the audience to look at and admire. As a matter of fact, there is just as much that is interesting, strange, mysterious, and wonderful; just as much to be learned that is edifying, broadening, and refining in a cabbage as there is in a page of Latin. There is, however, this distinction: it will make very little difference to the world whether one Negro boy, more or less, learns to construe a page of Latin. On the other hand, as soon as one Negro boy has been taught to apply thought and study and ideas to the growing of cabbages, he has started a process which, if it goes on and continues, will eventually transform the whole face of things as they exist in the South to-day.

I have spoken hitherto about industrial education as a means of connecting education with life. The mere fact that a boy has learned in school to handle a plane or that he has learned something about the chemistry of the soil does not of itself insure that he has gained any new and vital grip upon the life about him. He must at the same time learn to use the knowledge and the training that he has received to change and improve the conditions about him.

In my travels I have come across some very interesting and amusing examples of the failures of teachers to connect their teaching with real things, even when they had a chance right at hand to do so. I recall visiting, not long since, a somewhat noted school which has a department for industrial or hand training, concerning which the officers of the school had talked a great deal. Almost directly in front of the building used for the so-called industrial training—I noticed a large brick building in process of erection. In the construction of this building every principle of mechanics taught in the manual-training department of this institution was being put into actual use. Notwithstanding this fact, I learned upon inquiry that the teacher had made no attempt to connect what was taught in the manual-training department with the work on the brick building across the way. The students had no opportunity to work on this building; they had not visited it with their teacher; they had made no attempt to study the actual problems that had arisen in the course of its construction. As far as they were concerned, there was no relation whatever between the subjects discussed in the class room or the operations carried on in the school shops and the work that was going on outside. All that they were getting in the school was, as far as I was able to learn, just as formal in its character, just as much an educational ceremony, as if they were engaged in diagraming a sentence in English or reciting the parts of a Latin verb.

My experience in the little country school in West Virginia first taught me that it was possible to take teaching outside of the text-book and deal with real things. I have learned from later experience that it is just as important to carry education outside of the school building and take it into the fields, into the homes, and into the daily life of the people surrounding the school.

One of the most important activities of our school at Tuskegee is what we call our Extension Work, in which nearly all the departments of the Institute coöperate. In fact, at the present time more attention, energy, and effort are directed to this work outside the school grounds than to any other branch of work in which the school is engaged.

It would be impossible to describe here all the ramifications or all the various forms which this extension work has taken in recent years. The thing that I wish to emphasize, however, is that we are seeking in this work less to teach (according to the old-fashioned notion of teaching) than to improve conditions. We are trying to improve the methods of farming in the country surrounding the school, to change and improve the home life of the farming population, and to establish a model school system—not only for Macon but for several other counties in the state.

Perhaps I can best illustrate what I mean when I say that education should connect itself with life, by describing a type of rural school which we have worked out and are seeking to establish in Macon County. There are several schools in our county which might be called, in a certain sense, model country schools. There are nearly fifty communities in which, during the last four or five years, new school buildings have been erected and the school terms lengthened to eight and nine months, largely with funds collected from the Negro farmers under the direction and inspiration of the Tuskegee Institute.

The school that I have in mind is known as the "Rising Star." That is the name that the coloured people gave to their church, and that is now the name which has become

THE "RISING STAR" SCHOOLHOUSE

With which the community was once satisfied

THE "RISING STAR" SCHOOLHOUSE

That the changed conditions have produced

community. In addition to the ordinary reading book, pupils in this school spend some time every week reading a little local agricultural newspaper which is published at Tuskegee Institute in the interest of the farmers and schools in the surrounding country.

It is interesting to observe the effect of this teaching on the fathers and mothers of the children who attend this school. As soon as fathers discovered that their boys were learning in school to tell how much their pigs, cotton, and corn were worth, the fathers (who had been more or less disappointed with the results of the previous education) felt that the school was really worth something after all. When the girls began to ask their mothers to let them take *their* dresses to school so that they might learn to patch and mend them, these mothers began to get an entirely new idea of what school meant. Later, when these girls were taught to make simple garments in the school room, their mothers became still more interested. They began to attend the mothers' meetings, and before long there was a genuine enthusiasm in that community—not only for the school and its teachers, but for the household improvement that they taught. The teachers used their influence with the pupils first of all to start a crusade of whitewashing and general cleaning-up. Houses that had never known a coat of white-wash began to assume a neat and attractive appearance. Better than all else, under the inspiration of this school and of the other schools like it, the whole spirit of this community and the others throughout the county improved.

In a short time a little revolution has taken place in the material, educational, moral, and religious life of "Rising Star." The influence of the school has extended to the minister and to the church. At the present time the sermons that are preached in the church have a vital connection with the moral life of the community. I shall not soon forget one of my recent visits to the church. The minister chose for his text: "The earth is full of Thy riches," and, to illustrate his sermon, he placed on the platform beside the pulpit two bushels of prize corn which he himself had grown on his farm. When he came to expound his text he pointed with pride to his little agricultural exhibit as an indication of the real significance of this sentence from the Bible, which had never before had any definite meaning for him.

Education, such as I have attempted to describe, touches the life of the white man as well as that of the black man. By encouraging Negro farmers to buy land and improve their methods of agriculture, it has multiplied the number of small landowners and increased the tax value of the land. Recent investigations show that the number of Negro landowners in Macon County has grown more in the last five or six years than in the whole previous period since the abolition of slavery. Land that was selling for two and three dollars an acre five years ago is now worth fifteen and twenty dollars an acre. In many parts of the county large plantations have been broken up and sold in small tracts to Negro farmers. At the last annual meeting of the Coloured State Teachers' Association, at Birmingham, one teacher from Macon County reported that during the previous year she had organized a club among the farmers through which six hundred acres of land had been purchased in her community.

The struggles of the Negro farmer to lengthen the school term, and the competition among different local communities in the county in the work of building and equipping school buildings, has had the effect of leading the coloured people to think about all kinds of matters that concern the welfare of their local communities. For example, Law and Order Leagues have been organized

TWO TYPES OF COLOURED CHURCHES

throughout Macon County to assist in enforcing the prohibition law. I do not believe that there is a county in the state
where these laws are better enforced than they are in our
county at the present time. At the last sitting of the grand

jury, only seventeen indictments for all classes of offences were returned. The next session of the criminal court will have, I am told, the smallest docket in its history. I am convinced that there is not a county in that state with so large a Negro population that has so small a number of criminals.

Silently and almost imperceptibly, the work of education has gone on from year to year, slowly changing conditions—not only in Macon County, but, to a greater or less extent, in other parts of Alabama and of the South. Education of the kind that I have described has helped to diminish the cost of production on the farm and, at the same time, has steadily increased the wants of the farmers. In other words, it has enabled the Negro farmer to earn more money, and at the same time has given him a reason for doing so.

Farmers have learned to plant gardens, to keep hogs and chickens, and, as far as possible, to raise their own food and fodder. This has led them to increase and sometimes double the annual amount of their labour. Under former conditions, the Negro farmer did not work more than one hundred and fifty days in the year. Merely to plant and harvest the cotton crop—he did not need to do so.

In learning to raise his own provisions, the Negro farmer is no longer dependent to the same extent that he formerly was upon the landlord or the storekeeper. Under the old system the Negro farmer obtained his provisions (or "advances" as they are called) from the storekeeper on credit. In order to carry him through the year until the cotton crop was harvested, the storekeeper borrowed from the local banker. The local banker borrowed, in turn, from the bankers in the city, who, perhaps, obtained a portion of their money from the large money centres of the North. Every time this money passed from one hand to the other, the man who loaned collected toll from the man who borrowed. At the bottom, where the system connected up with the Negro farmer, the planter or storekeeper added something to the costs which had already accumulated—as a sort of insurance, and to pay the expenses of looking after his tenant and seeing that he did his work properly, All this sum, of course, was finally paid by the man on the soil.

The farmer who has become independent enough to raise his own provisions, or a large portion of them, does not need the supervision of his landlord in his farming operations. At the present time the majority of the Negro farmers in Macon County get their money directly from the bank and pay cash for their provisions. A number have money on deposit in the local banks. The bankers' capital and deposits have increased so that they are not so dependent as they once were upon foreign capital to aid them in carrying on the farming operations in the county.

I do not mean to say that all this has been effected as a direct result of education; I merely wish to point out how intimately the kind of education that we are trying to introduce does, in fact, touch all the fundamental interests of the community.

Naturally the influences that I have referred to do not end with the effects that I have already described. The results obtained have had a reflex influence upon the schools themselves. From the very beginning of my work at Tuskegee I saw that our problem was a double one. We had at first to work out a kind of education which would meet the needs of the masses of the coloured people. We had, in the second place, to convince the white people that education could be made of real value to the Negro.

There are many sincere and honest men in the South to-day who do not believe that education has done or will do the race any good. In my opinion, Negro education will never be an entire success in the South until it gets the sympathy and support of these men. Arguments will not go far toward convincing men like these. It is necessary to show them results.

The people in Macon County are not exceptional in this respect. Until a few years ago I think that I should have described the attitude of a majority of the white people in that county as indifferent. To-day I believe that I am safe in saying that nine tenths of the people of Macon County believe in Negro education.

Let me speak of some of the ways in which this attitude of the white people has manifested itself. In the first place, when a school house is to be built or some improvements to be made in the community where the white man lives, he contributes money toward it. One white man in Macon County recently gave $100 toward the erection of such a school. A number of white planters, who a few years ago were indifferent on the subject of Negro education, give annual prizes to the coloured people on their plantations. I know one planter who gives an annual prize to the Negro farmer who raises the largest number of bushels of corn on an acre of land. He gives another prize to the coloured family which keeps its children in the public school the greatest number of days during the year. He gives another prize to the woman who keeps her front yard in the best condition.

One of the white bankers in Macon County has established an annual prize to be given to the Negro farmer who raises the best oats on a given plot of land. The editor of the county paper gives an annual prize to the school in the county that has the best spelling class, the contest to take place at the annual Macon County Coloured Farmers' Fair.

At these fairs exhibitions are made of vegetables and grain raised by the children on the school farms. There are also exhibitions of cooking and sewing done by the children in the public schools of the county. Many of the white merchants and white farmers offer prizes for the best exhibition of agricultural products at this fair.

Gradually, as I have said, improved methods of educating the Negro are extending the same influences throughout the state of Alabama and the South. In fact, wherever a school is actually teaching boys and girls to do something that the community wants, it is seldom that that school fails to enlist the interest and coöperation of all the people in that community, whether they be black or white. This is, as definitely as I can express it, my own experience of the way in which educators can and do solve the race problem.

VII | COLONEL ROOSEVELT AND WHAT I HAVE LEARNED FROM HIM

SOME years ago—and not so very many, either—I think that I should have been perfectly safe in saying that the highest ambition of the average Negro in America was to hold some sort of office, or to have some sort of job that connected him with the Government. Just to be able to live in the capital city was a sort of distinction, and the man who ran an elevator or merely washed windows in Washington (particularly if the windows or the elevator belonged to the United States Government) felt that he was in some way superior to a man who cleaned windows or ran an elevator in any other part of the country. He felt that he was an office-holder!

There has been a great change in this respect in recent years. Many members of my race have learned that, in the long run, they can earn more money and be of more service to the community in almost any other position than that of an employé or office-holder under the Government. I know of a number of recent cases in which Negro business men have refused positions of honour and trust in the Government service because they did not care to give up their business interests. Notwithstanding, the city of Washington still has a peculiar attraction and even fascination for the average Negro.

I do not think that I ever shared that feeling of so many others of my race. I never liked the atmosphere of Washington. I early saw that it was impossible to build up a race of which the leaders were spending most of their time, thought, and energy in trying to get into office, or in trying to stay there after they were in. So, for the greater part of my life, I have avoided Washington; and even now I rarely spend a day in that city which I do not look upon as a day practically thrown away.

I do not like politics, and yet, in recent years, I have had some experience in political matters. However, no man who is in the least interested in public questions can escape some sort of connection with politics, I suppose, even if he does not want a political position. As a matter of fact, it was just because it was well known that I sought no political office of any kind and would accept no position with the Government, unless it were an honorary one, that brought my connection with politics about.

One thing that has taught me to dislike politics is the observation that, as soon as any person or thing becomes the subject of political discussion he or it at once assumes in the public mind an importance out of all proportion to his or its real merits. Time and time again I have seen a whole community (sometimes a whole county or state) wrought up to the highest pitch of excitement over the appointment of some person to a political position paying perhaps not more than $25 or $50 a month. At the same time I have seen individuals secure important positions at the head of a manufacturing house or receive an appointment to some important educational position that paid three or four times as much money (or perhaps purchase a farm), where just as much executive ability was required, without arousing public attention or causing comment in the newspapers. I have also seen white men and coloured men resign important positions in private life where they were earning much more than they could get under the Government, simply because of the false and mistaken ideas of the importance which they attached to a political position. All this has given me a distaste for political life.

In Mississippi, for example, a coloured man and his wife had charge, a few years ago, of a post-office. In some way or other a great discussion was started in regard to this case, and before long the whole community was in a state of excitement because coloured people held that position. A little later the post-office was given up and the coloured man, Mr. W. W. Cox, started a bank in the same town. At the present time he is the president of the bank and his wife assists him. As bankers they receive three or four times as much pay as they received from the post-office. The bank is patronized by both white and coloured people, and, when last I heard of it, was in a flourishing condition. As president of a Negro bank, Mr. Cox is performing a much greater service to the community than he could possibly render as postmaster. There are, no doubt, a great many people in his town who would be able to fill the position of postmaster, but there are very few who could start and successfully carry on an institution that would so benefit the community as a Negro bank. While he was postmaster, merely because his office was a political one, Mr. Cox occupied for some time the attention of the whole state of Mississippi; in fact, he (or rather his wife) was for a brief space almost a national figure. Now he is occupying a much more remunerative and important position in private life, but I do not think that he has attracted attention to amount to anything outside of the community in which he lives.

The effect of the excitement about this case has been greatly to exaggerate the importance of holding a Government position. The average Negro naturally feels that there must be some special value to him as an individual, as well as to his race, in holding a position which white people don't want him to hold, simply because he is a Negro. It leads him to believe that it is in some way more honourable or respectable to work for the Government as an official than for the community and himself as a private citizen.

Because of these facts, as well as for other reasons, I have never sought nor accepted a political position. During President Roosevelt's administration I was asked to go as a Commissioner of the United Sates to Liberia. In considering whether I should accept this position, it was urged that, because of the work that I had already done in this country for my own people and because my name was already known to some extent to the people of Liberia, I was the person best fitted to undertake the work that the Government wanted done. While I did not like the job and could ill spare the time from the work which I was trying to do for the people of my own race in America, I finally decided to accept the position. I was very happy, however, when President Taft kindly decided to relieve me from the necessity of making the trip and allowed my secretary, Mr. Emmett J. Scott, to go to Africa in my stead. This was as near as I ever came to holding a Government job. But there are other ways of getting into politics than by holding office.

In the case of the average man, it has seemed to me that as soon as he gets into office he becomes an entirely different man. Some men change for the better under the weight of responsibility; others change for the worse. I never could understand what there is in American politics that so fatally alters the character of a man. I have known men who, in their private life and in their business, were scrupulously careful to keep their word—men who would never, directly or indirectly, deceive any one with whom they were associated. When they took political office all this changed.

I once asked a coloured hack-driver in Washington how a certain coloured man whom I had known in private life (but who was holding a prominent office) was getting on. The old driver had little education but he was a judge of men, and he summed up the case in this way:

"Dere is one thing about Mr. ——; you can always depend on him." The old fellow shook his head and laughed. Then he added: "If he tells you he's gwine to do anything, you can always depend upon it that he's *not* gwine to do it."

This sort of change that comes over people after they get office is not confined, however, to the Negro race. Other races seem to suffer in the same way. I have seen men who, in the ordinary affairs of life, were cool and level headed, grow suspicious and jealous, give up interest in everything, neglect their business, sometimes even neglect their families; in short, lose entirely their mental and moral balance as soon as they started out in quest of an office.

I have watched these men after the political microbe attacked them, and I know all the symptoms of the disease that follows. They usually begin by carefully studying the daily newspapers. They attach great importance to the slightest thing that is said (or not said) by persons who they believe have political influence or authority. These men (the men who dispense the offices) soon come to assume an enormous importance in the minds of office-seekers. They watch all the movements of the political leaders with the

"LITTLE TEXAS" SCHOOLHOUSE, ALABAMA

Which has been replaced by a $600 building

"WASHINGTON MODEL SCHOOL," ALABAMA

With dwelling for its two teachers

greatest anxiety, and study every chance word that they let drop, as if it had some dark and awful significance. Then, when they get a little farther along, the office-seekers will, perhaps, be found tramping the streets, getting signatures of Tom, Dick, and Harry as a guarantee that they are best qualified to fill some office that they have in view.

I remember the case of a white man who lived in Alabama when President McKinley was first elected. This man gave up his business and went to Washington with a full determination to secure a place in the President's cabinet. He wrote me regularly concerning his prospects. After President McKinley had filled all the places in his cabinet, the same individual applied for a foreign ambasadorship; failing in that, he applied for an auditorhip in one of the departments; failing in that, he tried to get a clerkship in Washington; failing in that, he finally wrote to me (and to a number of other acquaintances in Alabama) and asked me to lend him enough money to defray his travelling expenses back to Alabama.

Of course, not all men who go into politics are affected in the way that I have described. Let me add that I have known many public men and have studied them carefully, but the best and highest example of a man that was the same in political office that he was in private life is Col. Theodore Roosevelt. He is not the only example, but he is the most conspicuous one in this respect that I have ever known.

I was thrown, comparatively early in my career, in contact with Colonel Roosevelt. He was just the sort of man to whom any one who was trying to do work of any kind for the improvement of any race or type of humanity would naturally go to for advice and help. I have seen him and been in close contact with him under many varying circumstances and I confess that I have learned much from studying his career, both while he was in office and since he has been in private life. One thing that impresses me about Mr. Roosevelt is that I have never known him, having given a promise, to overlook or forget it; in fact, he seems to forget nothing, not even the most trivial incidents. I found him the same when he was President that he was as a private citizen, or as Governor of New York, or as Vice-President of the United States. In fact, I have no hesitation in saying that I consider him the highest type of all-round man that I have ever met.

One of the most striking things about Mr. Roosevelt, both in private and public life, is his frankness. I have been often amazed at the absolute directness and candour of his speech. He does not seem to know how to hide anything. In fact, he seems to think aloud. Many people have referred to him as being impulsive and as acting without due consideration. From what I have seen of Mr. Roosevelt in this regard, I have reached the conclusion that what people describe as impulsiveness in him is nothing else but quickness of thought. While other people are thinking around a question, he thinks through it. He reaches his conclusions while other people are considering the preliminaries. He cuts across the field, as it were, in his methods of thinking. It is true that in doing so he often takes great chances and risks much. But Colonel Roosevelt is a man who never shrinks from taking chances when it is necessary to take them. I remember that, on one occasion, when it seemed to me that he had risked a great deal in pursuing a certain line of action, I suggested to him that it seemed to me that he had taken a great chance.

"One never wins a battle," he replied, "unless he takes some risks."

Another characteristic of Colonel Roosevelt, as compared with many other prominent men in public life, is that he rarely forgets or forsakes a friend. If a man once wins his confidence, he stands by that man. One always knows where to find him—and that, in my opinion, accounts to a large degree for his immense popularity. His friend, particularly if he happens to be holding a public position, may become very unpopular with the public, but unless that friend has disgraced himself, Mr. Roosevelt will always stand by him, and is not afraid or ashamed to do so. In the long run the world respects a man who has the courage to stand by his friends, whether in public or private life, and Mr. Roosevelt has frequently gained popularity by doing things that more discreet politicians would have been afraid to do.

I first became acquainted with Mr. Roosevelt through correspondence. Later, in one of my talks with him—and this was at a time when there seemed little chance of his ever becoming President, for it was before he had even been mentioned for that position—he stated to me in the frankest manner that some day he would like to be President of the United States. The average man, under such circumstances, would not have thought aloud. If he believed that there was a remote opportunity of gaining the Presidency, he would have said that he was not seeking the office; that his friends were thrusting it on him; that he did not have the ability to be President, and so forth. Not so with Colonel Roosevelt. He spoke out, as is his custom, that which was in his mind. Even then, many years before he attained his ambition, he began to outline to me how he wanted to help not only the Negro, but the whole South, should he ever become President. I question whether any man ever went into the Presidency with a more sincere desire to be of real service to the South than Mr. Roosevelt did.

That incident will indicate one of the reasons why Mr. Roosevelt succeeds. He not only thinks quickly, but he plans and thinks a long distance ahead. If he had an important state paper to write, or an important magazine article or speech to prepare, I have known him to prepare it six or eight months ahead. The result is that he is at all times master of himself and of his surroundings. He does not let his work push him; he pushes his work.

Practically everything that he tried to do for the South while he was President was outlined in conversations to me many years before it became known to most people that he had the slightest chance of becoming President. What he did was not a matter of impulse but the result of carefully matured plans.

An incident which occurred immediately after he became President will illustrate the way in which Mr. Roosevelt's mind works upon a public problem. After the death of President McKinley I received a letter from him, written in his own hand, on the very day that he took the oath of office at Buffalo as President—or was it the day following?—in which he asked me to meet him in Washington. He wanted to talk over with me the plans for helping the South that we had discussed years before. This plan had lain matured in his mind for months and years and, as soon as the opportunity came, he acted upon it.

When I received this letter from Mr. Roosevelt, asking me to meet him in Washington, I confess that it caused me some grave misgivings. I felt that I must consider seriously the question whether I should allow myself to be drawn into a kind of activity that I had definitely determined to keep away from. But here was a letter which, it seemed to me, I could not lightly put aside, no matter what my personal wishes or feelings might be. Shortly after Mr. Roosevelt became established in the White House I went there to see him and we spent the greater part of an evening in

talk concerning the South. In this conversation he emphasized two points in particular: First, he said that wherever he
appointed a white man to office in the South he wished
him to be the very highest type of native Southern white
man—one in whom the whole country had faith. He
repeated and emphasized his determination to appoint such
a type of man regardless of political influences or political
consequences.

Then he stated to me, quite frankly, that he did not propose to appoint a large number of coloured people, to office
in any part of the South, but that he did propose to do two
things which had not been done before that time—at least
not to the extent and with the definite purpose that he had
in mind. Wherever he did appoint a coloured man to office
in the South, he said that he wanted him to be not only a
man of ability, but of character—a man who had the confidence of his white and coloured neighbours. He did not
propose to appoint a coloured man to office simply for the
purpose of temporary political expediency. He added that,
while he proposed to appoint fewer coloured men to office
in the South, he proposed to put a certain number of
coloured men of high character and ability in office in the
Northern states. He said that he had never been able to see
any good reason why coloured men should be put in office
in the Southern states and not in the North as well.

As a matter of fact, before Mr. Roosevelt became President, not a single coloured man had ever been appointed, so
far as I know, to a Federal office in any Northern state. Mr.
Roosevelt determined to set the example by placing a
coloured man in a high office in his own home city, so that
the country might see that he did not want other parts of
the country to accept that which he himself was not willing
to receive. Some months afterward, as a result of this policy,

the Hon. Charles W. Anderson was made collector of internal revenues for the second district of New York. This is the district in which Wall Street is located and the district that receives, perhaps, more revenue than any other in the United States. Later on, Mr. Roosevelt appointed other coloured men to high office in the North and West, but I think that any one who examines into the individual quali- fications of the coloured men appointed to office by Mr. Roosevelt will find, in each case, that they were what he insisted that they should be—men of superior ability and of superior character.

President Taft happily has followed the same policy. He has appointed Whitefield McKinlay, of Washington, to the collectorship of the port of Georgetown, a position which has never heretofore been held by a black man. He had des- ignated J. C. Napier, cashier of the One-Cent Savings Bank of Nashville, Tenn., to serve as register of the United States treasury; and he has recently announced the appointment of William H. Lewis, assistant United States district attorney, Boston, Mass., to the highest appointive position ever held by a black man under the Federal Government, namely, to a place as assistant attorney general of the United States.

Back of their desire to improve the public service, Mr. Roosevelt and Mr. Taft have had another purpose in appointing to office the kind of coloured people that I have named. They have said that they desire the persons appointed by them to be men of the highest character in order that the younger generation of coloured people might see that men of conspicuous ability and conspicuous purity of character are recognized in politics as in other walks of life. They have hoped that such recognition might lead other coloured people to strive to attain a high reputation.

Mr. Roosevelt did not apply this rule to the appointments of coloured people alone. He believed that he could not only greatly improve the public service, but to some extent could change the tone of politics in the South and improve the relations of the races by the appointment of men who stood high in their professions and who were not only friendly to the coloured people but had the confidence of the white people as well. These men, he hoped, would be to the South a sort of model of what the Federal Government desired and expected of its officials in their relations with all parties.

During the first conference with Mr. Roosevelt in the White House, after discussing many matters, he finally agreed to appoint a certain white man, whose name had been discussed, to an important judicial position. Within a few days the appointment was made and accepted. I question whether any appointment made in the South has ever attracted more attention or created more favourable comment from people of all classes than was true of this one.

During the fall of 1901, while I was making a tour of Mississippi, I received word to the effect that the President would like to have a conference with me, as soon as it was convenient, concerning some important matters. With a friend, who was travelling with me, I discussed very seriously the question whether, with the responsibilities I already had, I should take on others. After considering the matter carefully, we decided that the only policy to pursue was to face the new responsibilities as they arose, because new responsibilities bring new opportunities for usefulness of which I ought to take advantage in the interest of my race. I was the more disposed to feel that this was a duty because Mr. Roosevelt was proposing to carry out the very policies which I had advocated ever since I began work in Alabama. Immediately after finishing my work in Mississippi I went to Washington. I arrived there in the afternoon and went to the house of a friend, Mr. Whitefield McKinlay, with whom I was expected to stop during my stay in Washington.

This trip to Washington brings me to a matter which I have hitherto constantly refused to discuss in print or in public, though I have had a great many requests to do so. At the time, I did not care to add fuel to the controversy which it aroused, and I speak of it now only because it seems to me that an explanation will show the incident in its true light and in its proper proportions.

When I reached Mr. McKinlay's house I found an invitation from President Roosevelt asking me to dine with him at the White House that evening at eight o'clock. At the hour appointed I went to the White House and dined with the President and members of his family and a gentleman from Colorado. After dinner we talked at considerable length concerning plans about the South which the President had in mind. I left the White House almost immediately and took a train the same night for New York. When I reached New York the next morning I noticed that the New York *Tribune* had about two lines stating that I had dined with the President the previous night. That was the only New York paper, so far as I saw, that mentioned the matter. Within a few hours the whole incident completely passed from my mind. I mentioned the matter casually, during the day, to a friend—Mr. William H. Baldwin, Jr., then president of the Long Island Railroad—but spoke of it to no one else and had no intention of doing so. There was, in fact, no reason why I should discuss it or mention it to any one.

My surprise can be imagined when, two or three days afterward, the whole press, North and South, was filled with despatches and editorials relating to my dinner with the

President. For days and weeks I was pursued by reporters in quest of interviews. I was deluged with telegrams and letters asking for some expression of opinion or an explanation; but during the whole of this period of agitation and excitement I did not give out a single interview and did not discuss the matter in any way.

Some newspapers attempted to weave into this incident a deliberate and well-planned scheme on the part of President Roosevelt to lead the way in bringing about the social intermingling of the two races. I am sure that nothing was farther from the President's mind than this; certainly it was not in my mind. Mr. Roosevelt simply found that he could spare the time best during and after the dinner hour for the discussion of the matters which both of us were interested in.

The public interest aroused by this dinner seemed all the more extraordinary and uncalled for because, on previous occasions, I had taken tea with Queen Victoria at Windsor Castle; I had dined with the governors of nearly every state in the North; I had dined in the same room with President McKinley at Chicago at the Peace-jubilee dinner; and I had dined with ex-President Harrison in Paris, and with many other prominent public men.

Some weeks after the incident I was making a trip through Florida. In some way it became pretty generally known along the railroad that I was on the train, and the result was that at nearly every station a group of people would get aboard and shake hands with me. At a little station near Gainesville, Fla., a white man got aboard the train whose dress and manner indicated that he was from the class of small farmers in that part of the country. He shook hands with me very cordially, and said:

"I am mighty glad to see you. I have heard about you and I have been wanting to meet you for a long while."

I was naturally pleased at this cordial reception, but I was surprised when, after looking me over, he remarked: "Say, you are a great man. You are the greatest man in this country!"

I protested mildly, but he insisted, shaking his head and repeating, "Yes, sir, the greatest man in this country." Finally I asked him what he had against President Roosevelt, telling him at the same time that, in my opinion, the President of the United States was the greatest man in the country.

"Huh! Roosevelt?" he replied with considerable emphasis in his voice. "I used to think that Roosevelt was a great man until he ate dinner with you. That settled him for me."

This remark of a Florida farmer is but one of the many experiences which have taught me something of the curious nature of this thing that we call prejudice—social prejudice, race prejudice, and all the rest. I have come to the conclusion that these prejudices are something that it does not pay to disturb. It is best to "let sleeping dogs lie." All sections of the United States, like all other parts of the world, have their own peculiar customs and prejudices. For that reason it is the part of common-sense to respect them. When one goes to European countries or into the Far West, or into India or China, he meets certain customs and certain prejudices which he is bound to respect and, to a certain extent, comply with. The same holds good regarding conditions in the North and in the South. In the South it is not the custom for coloured and white people to be entertained at the same hotel; it is not the custom for black and white children to attend the same school. In most parts of the North a different custom prevails. I have never stopped to question or quarrel with the customs of the people in the part of the country in which I found myself.

Thus, in dining with President Roosevelt, there was no disposition on my part—and I am sure there was no disposition on Mr. Roosevelt's part—to attack any custom of the South. There is, therefore, absolutely no ground or excuse for the assertion sometimes made that our dining together was part of a preconcerted and well-thought-out plan. It was merely an incident that had no thought or motive behind it except the convenience of the President.

I was born in the South and I understand thoroughly the prejudices, the customs, the traditions of the South—and, strange as it may seem to those who do not wholly understand the situation, I love the South. There is no Southern white man who cherishes a deeper interest than I in everything that promotes the progress and the glory of the South. For that reason, if for no other, I will never willingly and knowingly do anything that, in my opinion, will provoke bitterness between the races or misunderstanding between the North and the South.

Now that the excitement in regard to it is all over, it may not be out of place, perhaps, for me to recall the famous order disbanding a certain portion of the Twenty-fifth Infantry (a Negro regiment) because of the outbreak at Brownsville, Texas, particularly since this is an illustration of the trait in Mr. Roosevelt to which I have referred. I do not mind stating here that I did not agree with Mr. Roosevelt's method of punishing the Negro soldiers, even supposing that they were guilty. In his usual frank way, he told me several days prior to issuing that order what he was going to do. I urged that he find some other method of punishing the soldiers. While, in some matters, I was perhaps instrumental in getting him to change an opinion that he had formed, in this case he told me that his mind was perfectly clear and that he had reached a definite decision which he would not change, because he was certain that he was right.

At the time this famous order was issued there was no

man in the world who was so beloved by the ten millions of Negroes in America as Colonel Roosevelt. His praises were sung by them on every possible occasion. He was their idol. Within a few days—I might almost say hours—as a consequence of this order, the songs of praise of ten millions of people were turned into a chorus of criticism and censure.

Mr. Roosevelt was over and over again urged and besought by many of his best friends, both white and coloured, to modify or change this order. Even President Taft, who was at that time Secretary of War, urged him to withdraw the order or modify it. I urged him to do the same thing. He stood his ground and refused. He said that he was convinced that he was right and that events would justify his course.

Nothwithstanding the fact that I was deeply concerned in the outcome of this order, I confess that I could not but admire the patience with which Mr. Roosevelt waited for the storm to blow over. I do not think that the criticisms and denunciation which he received had the effect of swerving him in the least from the general course that he had determined to pursue with regard to the coloured people of the country. He was just as friendly in his attitude to them after the Brownsville affair as before.

Months have passed since the issuing of the order; the agitation has subsided and the bitterness has disappeared. I think that I am safe in saying that, while the majority of coloured people still feel that Colonel Roosevelt made a mistake in issuing the order, there is no individual who is more popular and more loved by the ten millions of Negroes in America than he.

VIII | MY EDUCATIONAL CAMPAIGNS THROUGH THE SOUTH AND WHAT THEY TAUGHT ME

SEVERAL years ago, in company with a few personal friends, most of them Negro business men of Little Rock, Ark., I made a week's journey through Arkansas and Oklahoma, visiting most of the principal cities, speaking, wherever I had time and opportunity along the route, to audiences of both races.

In order to cover as much ground as possible in the eight days we had allotted to the trip, and in order to make the journey as comfortable as possible, we secured a special car in St. Louis and on the night of November 17, 1905, I think it was, we started out on what was one of the most interesting and memorable journeys I have ever made.

For several years my friend, Mr. John E. Bush, receiver of public moneys at Little Rock, and at that time head of the local Negro Business League in that city, had been urging me to come and see for myself the progress which Negroes were making in Little Rock and the neighbouring city of Pine Bluff. After I had finally decided to accept his invitation, I made up my mind that I would take advantage of the opportunity to see something, also, of the progress

Negroes were making in the neighbouring state of Oklahoma and in what was then the Indian Territory.

At that time thousands of Negroes were pouring into this new country from the South. Some of my own students were either in business or teaching school in different parts of the present state of Oklahoma and from them, and from other sources, I had heard much of the progress that coloured people were making, particularly at Muskogee and in the booming little Negro town of Boley, where, within a few years, a flourishing little city, controlled entirely by Negroes, and without a single white inhabitant, had sprung into existence.

In the course of my journey I visited not only Little Rock and Pine Bluff, Ark., but Oklahoma City, Guthrie, Muskogee, South McAlester, and several other towns in Oklahoma, and I confess that I was surprised to note the enterprise which these coloured immigrants had shown and the progress they were making, particularly in material and business directions. I met successful farmers, who, having sold their farms in Texas or in Kansas at a considerable advance, had come out into this new country to re-invest their money. I made the acquaintance in nearly every part of the state, of successful merchants, bankers, and professional men. At South McAlester I stayed at the home of E. E. McDaniels, a successful railway contractor, the first Negro I ever happened to meet who was engaged in that business. At Oklahoma City I remember meeting Albert Smith, who is known out there as the "Negro cotton king" because he gained the prize at the Paris Exposition in 1900 for the best bale of cotton. It was a great satisfaction to me to be able to talk with these men, to hear from their own lips the stories of their struggles, of their difficulties, mistakes, and successes. It seemed to me that, after talking with them around the fireside and in the close and intimate way I have suggested, I gained a deeper insight into the forces that were making for the upbuilding of my race than I could have possibly gained in any other way.

One thing that particularly impressed me was the difference between the condition of the coloured people who were pouring into this new portion of the Southwest and the condition of those who some thirty years before had poured into Kansas at the time of the famous "exodus." At that time some forty thousand bewildered and helpless coloured people, coming for the most part from the plantations of Louisiana, Arkansas, and Mississippi, made their way to Kansas in the hope of finding there greater opportunity and more freedom. It was people from these same regions who, with much the same purpose, were at this time pouring into Oklahoma. The difference was that these later immigrants came with a definite notion of where they were going; they brought a certain amount of capital with them, and had a pretty clear idea of what they would find and what they proposed to do when they reached their destination. The difference in these two movements of the population seemed to me the most striking indication I had seen of the progress which the masses of the Negro people had made in a little more than thirty years.

During the next five years, in company with different parties of Negro business and professional men, I made similar journeys of observation through Mississippi, Tennessee, South Carolina, North Carolina, Delaware, and portions of Virginia and West Virginia. In several instances we made use of special trains to make these trips, and this enabled us to cover longer distances and make the journey practically on our own time. On each of these journeys I took advantage of my opportunities, not only to meet and talk with the

MR. WASHINGTON ADDRESSING AN AUDIENCE OF VIRGINIA NEGROES

people individually, but also to speak to large audiences of white and coloured people about many matters which concerned the interests of both races and particularly about the importance, to both races, of increasing the efficiency of the Negro schools. In fact, I had not made more than two or three of these trips before they came to be regarded by both white and coloured people as the beginning, in each of the states I visited, of a movement or campaign in the interest of Negro education.

Perhaps I can best indicate the character of these campaigns and the sort of information and insight that they gave me in regard to the condition of the coloured people in the states I visited by giving a more extended account of my journey in Mississippi in 1908. As an indication of the general interest in the purpose and the success of my visit I ought to say that, while the journey was made under the direction of the Negro Business League of Mississippi, representatives of nearly every important interest among Negroes in the state either accompanied the party for a portion of the journey or assisted in making the meetings successful at the different places at which we stopped. For instance, as I remember, there were not less than eight presidents of Negro banks and many other successful business men in the course of the eight-day trip. Among them were Charles Banks, president of the Negro Business League of Mississippi, and one of the most influential coloured men of the state. It was he who was more directly responsible than any one else for organizing and making a success of our journey. Not only the business men, but the representatives of different religious denominations and of the secret organizations, which are particularly strong in Mississippi, united with the members of the business league to make the meetings which we held in the different parts of the state as successful and as influential as it was possible to make them.

It is a matter of no small importance to the success of the people of my race in Mississippi that business men, teachers, and the members of the different religious denominations are uniting disinterestedly in the effort to give the coloured children of the state a proper and adequate education, and that they are using their influence to encourage the masses of the people to get property and build homes.

Dr. E. C. Morris, for instance, who was a member of the party, represents the largest Negro organization of any kind in the world—the National Baptist Convention, which has a membership of more than two millions; J. W. Straughter, as a member of the finance committee of the Negro Pythians, represented an organization of about seventy thousand persons, owning about three hundred and twenty-two thousand dollars' worth of property. The *African Methodist Episcopal Review*, of which Dr. H. T. Kealing, now president of the Negro college at Quindaro, Kan., is editor, is probably the best-edited and one of the most influential periodicals published by the Negro race. It has been in existence now for more than twenty-five years.

I have mentioned the names of these men and have referred to their positions and influence among the Negro people as showing how widespread at the present time is the interest in the moral and material upbuilding of the race.

I had heard a great deal, indirectly, before I reached Mississippi, of the progress that the coloured people were making there. I had also heard a great deal through the newspapers of the difficulties under which they were labouring. There are some portions of Mississippi, for instance, where a large part of the coloured population has been driven out as a result of white-capping organizations. There are other portions of the state where the white people and the coloured people seem to be getting along as well as, if not better than, in any other portion of the Union.

After leaving Memphis, the first place at which we stopped was Holly Springs, in Marshall County. Holly Springs has long been an educational centre for the coloured people of Mississippi. Shortly after the war the Freedman's Aid and Southern Educational Society of the Methodist Church established here Rust University. Until a few years ago the State Normal School for Training Negro Teachers was in existence in Holly Springs, when it was finally abolished by former Governor Vardaman. The loss of this school was a source of great disappointment to the coloured people of the state, as they felt that, in vetoing the appropriation, the governor was making an attack upon the Negro education of the state. Under the leadership of Bishop Cottrell, a new industrial school and theological seminary has grown up to take the place of the Normal Training School and do its work. During the previous two years Bishop Cottrell had succeeded in raising more than seventy-five thousand dollars, largely from the coloured people of Mississippi, in order to erect the two handsome modern buildings which form the nucleus of the new school. In this city there had also been recently established a Baptist Normal School, which is the contribution of the Negro Baptists of the state in response to the abolition of the State Normal School.

The enthusiasm for education that I discovered at Holly Springs is merely an indication of the similar enthusiasm in every other part of the state that I visited. At Utica, Miss., I spoke in the assembly room of the Utica Institute, founded October 27, 1903, by William H. Holtzclaw, a graduate of Tuskegee. After leaving Tuskegee he determined to go to the part of the country where it seemed to him that the coloured people were most in need of a school that could be conducted along the lines of Tuskegee Institute. He settled in Hinds County, where there are forty thousand coloured people, thirteen thousand of whom can neither read nor write. In the community in which this school was started the Negroes outnumber the whites seven to one. He began teaching out in the forests. From the very first he succeeded in gaining the sympathy of both races for the work that he was trying to do. In the five years since the school started he has succeeded in purchasing a farm of fifteen hundred acres. He had at that time erected three large and eleven small buildings of various kinds for school rooms, shops, and homes. On the farm there were one large plantation house and about thirty farm houses. He told me that a conservative estimate of the property which the school owned would make the valuation something more than seventy-five thousand dollars. In addition to this, he has already started an endowment fund in order to make the work that he is doing there permanent, and to give aid by means of scholarships to worthy students who are not fully able to pay their own way.

At Jackson, Miss., there are two colleges for Negro students. Campbell College was founded by the African Methodist Episcopal Church; Jackson College, which had just opened a handsome new building for the use of its students, was established and is supported by the Baptist denomination. At Natchez I was invited to take part in the dedication of the beautiful new building erected by the Negro Baptists of Mississippi at a cost of about twenty thousand dollars.

Perhaps I ought to say that, while there has been considerable rivalry among the different Negro churches along theological lines, it seems to me that I can see that, as the leaders of the people begin to realize the seriousness of the educational problem, this rivalry is gradually dying out in a disinterested effort to educate the masses of the Negro children irrespective of denominations. The so-called denominational schools are merely a contribution of the members of the different sects to the education of the race.

Nothing indicates the progress which the coloured people have made along material lines so well as the number of banks that have been started by coloured people in all parts of the South. I have made a special effort recently to learn something of the influence of these institutions upon the mass of the coloured people. At the present time there are no less than fifty-six Negro banks in the United States. All but one or two of them are in the Southern States. Of these fifty-six banks, eleven are in the state of Mississippi. Not infrequently I have found that Negro banks owe their existence to the secret and fraternal organizations. There are forty-two of these organizations, for example, in the state of Mississippi, and they collected $708,670 in 1907, and paid losses to the amount of $522,757. Frequently the banks have been established to serve as depositories for the funds of these institutions. They have then added a savings department, and have done banking business for an increasing number of stores and shops of various kinds that have been established within the last ten years by Negro business men.

A special study of the city of Jackson, Miss., made shortly before I visited the city, showed that there were ninety-three businesses conducted by Negroes in that city. Of this number, forty-four concerns did a total annual business of about three hundred and eighty-eight thousand dollars a year. But, of this amount of business, one contractor alone did one hundred thousand dollars' worth. As near as could be estimated, about 73 per cent. of the coloured people owned or were buying their own homes. It is said that the Negroes, who make up one half of the population, own one third of the area of the city of Jackson. The value of this property, however, is only about one eleventh of the taxable value of the city.

As nearly as could be estimated at that time, Negroes had on deposit in the various banks of the city almost two hundred thousand dollars. Of this amount, more than seventy thousand was in the two Negro banks of the city. I learned that most of these businesses had been started in the previous ten years, but, as a matter of fact, one of the oldest business men in Jackson is a coloured man, with whom I stopped during my visit to that city. H. T. Risher is the leading business man in his particular line in Jackson. He has had a bakery and restaurant in that city, as I understand, for more than twenty years. He has one of the handsomest of the many beautiful residences of coloured people in Jackson, which I had an opportunity to visit on my journey through the state.

Among the other business enterprises that especially attracted my attention during my journey was the drug store and offices of Dr. A. W. Dumas, of Natchez. His store is located in a handsome two-story brick block, and although there are a large number of Negro druggists in the United States, I know of no store which is better kept and makes a more handsome appearance.

According to the plan of our journey, I was to spend seven days in Mississippi, starting from Memphis, Tenn., going thence to Holly Springs, Utica, Jackson, Natchez, Vicksburg, Greenville, Mound Bayou, and then, crossing the Mississippi, to spend Sunday in the city of Helena, Ark. As a matter of fact, we did stop at other places and I had an opportunity to speak to audiences of coloured people and white people at various places along the railroad, the conductor kindly holding the train for me to do this at several points, so that I think it is safe to say that I spoke to forty or fifty thousand people during the eight days of our journey. Everywhere, I found the greatest interest and enthusiasm among both the white people and coloured people for the work that we were attempting to do. In Jackson, which for a number of years had been the centre of agitation upon the Negro question, there was some opposition expressed to the white people of the town attending the meeting, but I was told that among the people in the audience were Governor Noel; Lieutenant-Governor Manship; Major R. W. Milsaps, who is said to be the wealthiest man in Mississippi; Bishop Charles B. Galloway, of the Methodist Episcopal Church (South), who has since died; United States Marshal Edgar S. Wilson; the postmaster of Jackson, and a number of other prominent persons.

At Natchez the white people were so interested in the object of the meeting that they expressed a desire to pay for the opera house in which I spoke, provided that the seating capacity should be equally divided between the two races. At Vicksburg I spoke in a large building that had been used for some time for a roller-skating rink. I was informed that hundreds of people who wished to attend the meeting were unable to find places. At Greenville I delivered an address in the court-house; and there were so many people who were unable to attend the address that, at the suggestion of the sheriff, I delivered a second one from the steps of the court-house.

The largest and most successful meeting of the trip was held at Mound Bayou, a town founded and controlled entirely by Negroes. This town, also, is the centre of a Negro colony of about three thousand people. Negroes own thirty thousand acres of land in direct proximity to the town. Mound Bayou is in the centre of the Delta district, where the coloured people outnumber the whites frequently as much as ten to one; and there are a number of Negro settlements besides Mound Bayou in which no white man lives. My audience extended out into the surrounding fields as far as my voice could reach. I was greatly impressed with the achievements and possibilities of this town, where Negroes are giving a striking example of success in self-government and in business.

From what I was able to see during my visit to Mississippi, and from what I have been able to learn from other sources, I have come to the conclusion that more has been accomplished by the coloured people of that state during the last ten years than was accomplished by them during the whole previous period since the Civil War. To a large extent this has been due to the fact that the coloured people have learned that in getting land, in building homes, and in saving their money they can make themselves a force in the com-

munities in which they live. It is generally supposed that the
coloured man, in his efforts to rise, meets more opposition
in Mississippi than anywhere else in the United States, but
it is quite as true that there, more than anywhere else, the
coloured people seem to have discovered that, in gaining
habits of thrift and industry, in getting property, and in
making themselves useful, there is a door of hope open for
them which the South has no disposition to close.

As an illustration of what I mean, I may say that while I
was in Holly Springs I learned that, though the whites out-
numbered the blacks nearly three to one in Marshall
County, there had been but one lynching there since the
Civil War. When I inquired of both white people and
coloured people why it was that the two races were able to
live on such friendly terms, both gave almost exactly the
same answer. They said that it was due to the fact that in
Marshall County so large a number of coloured farmers
owned their farms. Among other things that have doubtless
helped to bring about this result is the fact that the treasurer
of the Odd Fellows of Mississippi, who lived in Holly
Springs, frequently had as much as two hundred thousand
dollars on deposit in the local banks.

My purpose in making the educational campaigns to
which I have referred was not merely to see the condition
of the masses of my own people, but to ascertain, also, the
actual relations existing between the races and to say a word
if possible that would bring about more helpful relations
between white men and black men in the communities
which I visited.

Again and again in the course of these journeys I
noticed that, almost invariably, as soon as I began to inquire
of some coloured school teacher, merchant, banker, physi-
cian, how it was he had gotten his start, each one began at

once to tell me of some prominent white man in their town who had befriended them. This man had advised them in their business transactions, had, perhaps, loaned them money, or had pointed out to them where they could invest their savings to advantage, and in this way had managed to get ahead. In some cases the very men who had privately befriended these individual coloured men were persons who in their public life had the reputation, outside of the community in which they lived, of being the violent opponents and enemies of the Negro race.

These experiences have been repeated so often in my journeys through the South that I have learned that public speeches and newspaper reports are a very poor indication of the actual relations of the races. Somehow when a Southern politician gets upon a platform to make a public speech it comes perfectly natural to him to denounce the Negro. He has been doing it so long that it is second nature.

Now one of the advantages of the educational campaigns I have described is that they have given an opportunity to Southern men to stand up in public and say what was deep down in their hearts with regard to the Negro, to express a feeling toward the Negro that represents another and higher side of Southern character and one which, as a result of sectional feelings and political controversies, has been too long hidden from the world.

After returning from my last educational trip through North Carolina I received letters from prominent people in all parts of the state expressing their approval of what I had said and of the work that my visit was intended to accomplish. These letters came from business men, from men who were or had been in public life, as well as from school superintendents. For example, Charles L. Coon, superintendent of public schools at Wilson, N.C., whose paper before the edu-

cational conference in Atlanta, in 1909, was the most convincing plea for the Negro schools I have ever read, wrote
as follows:

> I write to express my personal appreciation of your visit
> and its effects here in Wilson. You had a good audience
> representing all classes of our white and coloured popu-
> lation. Numbers of the best white people in town have
> told me that your address was the very best ever made
> here. Many of them say you must come back. Some want
> to get a warehouse so that everybody can hear you.
>
> The Negro school here is stronger in the affections
> of the coloured people, the white people are prouder of
> it, than before you came. I was delighted that we had a
> school building in which you could speak. The Negro
> school will get better each year. It is not doing nearly all
> it ought to do, but we are moving forward. There will be
> slight opposition from now on. I am more than ever con-
> vinced that white people will believe in and stand for the
> education of the Negro children, if the matter is put to
> them in the right shape. Our Negro school has more
> coloured than white opposition. In fact, the last white
> man in town who counts *one* was converted by you! I
> rejoice over this sinner's making his peace with me.

I have quoted Superintendent Coon's letter because it
represents the attitude toward Negro education and toward
the Negro of an increasing number of thoughtful and
earnest men of the younger generation in the South. Perhaps I can give no better idea of how many of the older
generation of the Southerners feel toward the Negro than
by quoting the words of Judge Bond, of Brownsville, Tenn.,
in the course of a few remarks he made at the close of my
address in his city.

Judge Bond said, according to a short-hand report taken at the time and afterward published in the Boston *Transcript*:

I was born and reared here in the South and have been associated all my life with Negroes. I feel that as a Southern white man I owe a debt to the Negro that I can never pay, that no Southern white man can ever pay. During the war the Southern white man left his home, his wife, and his children to be taken care of by the Negroes, and I have yet to hear of a single instance where that trust was betrayed or where they proved unfaithful; and ever since that time I have sworn by the Most Divine that I shall ever be grateful to the coloured people as long as I shall live, and that I shall never be unfair to that race. I have always since thought that a white man is not a man who does not admit that he owes a duty in the sight of God to the coloured people of this country; he is not a man if he is not willing at all times and under all circumstances to do all he can to acquit himself of that duty. If there was ever a people in this country who owed a debt to any people, it is the Southern white man to the Southern coloured man. The white man who lives on the other side of the Ohio River owes him a debt, too, but, by my honest conviction in the sight of God, his obligation is nothing compared to that of the Southern white man to the coloured people, and I have often wondered what will be the judgment on the Southern white man and his children and his grandchildren in failing to discharge his duty toward the old Negro, his children, and his grandchildren for their many years' faithful and true service.

My mother died at my birth. Now I am growing old. An old black mammy, who, thank God, is living to-day, took me in her arms and nursed me and cared for me and loved me until I grew strong and to manhood; and there has never been a day since that she has not been willing to do the same for my wife and children, even in spite of her years.

I remember some time ago very well, when I was sitting in a darkened room nursing my youngest child, who was confined with the dreaded disease small-pox, my wife in a most distressing manner appeared at the head of the stairs (we had been separated because of our little girl's condition and we were kept from the rest of the family upstairs). My wife called down to me and informed me that she feared another of our children had fallen victim to the small-pox. We were in a predicament, you may easily see. It was necessary at once to remove the child from the rest, but there still remained a doubt as to her being a victim, so we could not bring her into the room in which we were and it was also necessary that she be taken out of the room in which she was. She must be kept in a separate room and neither was it safe for her mother or myself to be in the room in which she would be taken. She must remain in this room all night without care or attention from either, but just about that time the old black mammy, this same black mammy who nursed and cared for me, appeared. Black mammy was heard from. "Small-pox or no small-pox, that child cannot stay in that room by herself to-night or no other night, even if I takes the small-pox and dies to-morrow"; and she did go into that room and stayed in that room until morning, and was willing to stay there as long as it was necessary. God bless her old soul!

I am glad to see Mr. Washington here and to have him speak to us. He is a credit to his race, and would be a credit to any race. I wish we had many more men like him all over this country.

Mr. Washington, I pray to God that the Spirit may ever guide you in your purpose to lift up your people and that you may inspire all Southern white men as well as Southern coloured men to lift up and elevate your race.

These expressions of interest in the welfare of my race and of hearty sympathy with work which others and myself have been trying to do for the upbuilding of the Negro have come to me in recent years from every part of the South. Almost from the beginning of my work in Alabama, however, I have had the support and the encouragement, both public and private, not only of my neighbours, but of the best white people everywhere in the South who were acquainted with what I was trying to do. When I have been inclined to be discouraged, the expressions of good-will have given me faith. They have taught me—in spite of wrongs and injustices to which members of my race are frequently subjected—to look with confidence to the future and to believe that the Negro has the power within himself to become an indispensable part of the life of the South, not feared and merely tolerated, but trusted and respected by the members of the white race by whom he is surrounded.

IX

WHAT I HAVE LEARNED FROM BLACK MEN

N O SINGLE question is more often asked me than this: "Has the pure blooded black man the same ability or the same worth as those of mixed blood?"

It has been my good fortune to have had a wide acquaintance with black as well as brown and even white Negroes. The race to which I belong permits me to meet and know people of all colours and conditions. There is no race or people who have within themselves the choice of so large a variety of colours and conditions as is true of the American Negro. The Japanese, as a rule, can know intimately human nature in only one hue, namely, yellow. The white man, as a rule, does not get intimately acquainted with any other than white men. The Negro, however, has a chance to know them all, because within his own race and among his own acquaintances he has friends, perhaps even relatives, of every colour in which mankind has been painted.

Perhaps I can answer the question as to the relative value of the pure Negro and the mixed blood in no better way than by telling what I know concerning, and what I have

learned from, some four or five men of the purest blood and
the darkest skins of any human beings I happen to know—
men to whom I am indebted for many things, but most of
all for what they have done for me in teaching me to value
all men at their real worth regardless of race or colour.

Among those black men whom I have known, the one
who comes first to my mind is Charles Banks, of Mound
Bayou, Miss., banker, cotton broker, planter, real-estate dealer,
head of a hundred-thousand-dollar corporation which is
erecting a cottonseed oil mill, the first ever built and controlled by Negro enterprise and Negro capital, and, finally,
leading citizen of the little Negro town of Mound Bayou.

I first met Charles Banks in Boston. As I remember, he
came in company with Hon. Isaiah T. Montgomery, the
founder of Mound Bayou, to represent, at the first meeting
of the National Negro Business League in 1900, the first
and at that time the only town in the United States
founded, inhabited, and governed exclusively by Negroes.
He was then, as he is to-day, a tall, big-bodied man, with a
shiny round head, quick, snapping eyes, and a surprisingly
swift and quiet way of reaching out and getting anything he
happens to want. I never appreciated what a big man Banks
was until I began to notice the swift and unerring way in
which he reached out his long arm to pick up, perhaps a
pin, or to get hold of the buttonhole and of the attention of
an acquaintance. He seemed to be able to reach without
apparent effort anything he wanted, and I soon found there
was a certain fascination in watching him move.

I have been watching Banks reach for things that he
wanted, and get them, ever since that time. I have been
watching him do things, watching him grow, and as I have
studied him more closely my admiration for this big, quiet,
graceful giant has steadily increased. One thing that has

always impressed itself upon me in regard to Mr. Banks is the fact that he never claims credit for doing anything that he can give credit to other people for doing. He has never made any effort to make himself prominent. He simply prefers to get a job done and, if he can use other people and give them credit for doing the work, he is happy to do so.

At the present time Charles Banks is not, by any means, the wealthiest, but I think I am safe in saying that he is the most influential, Negro business man in the United States. He is the leading Negro banker in Mississippi, where there are eleven Negro banks, and he is secretary and treasurer of the largest benefit association in that state, namely, that attached to the Masonic order, which paid death claims in 1910 to the amount of one hundred and ninety-five thousand dollars and had a cash balance of eighty thousand dollars. He organized and has been the moving spirit in the state organization of the Business League in Mississippi and has been for a number of years the vice-president of the National Negro Business League.

Charles Banks is, however, more than a successful business man. He is a leader of his race and a broad-minded and public-spirited citizen. Although he holds no public office, and, so far as I know, has no desire to do so, there are, in my opinion, few men, either white or black, in Mississippi today who are performing, directly or indirectly, a more important service to their state than Charles Banks.

Without referring to the influence that he has been able to exercise in other directions, I want to say a word about the work he is doing at Mound Bayou for the Negro people of the Yazoo Delta, where, in seventeen counties, the blacks represent from seventy-five to ninety-four per cent. of the whole population.

As I look at it, Mound Bayou is not merely a town; it is

at the same time and in a very real sense of that word, a school. It is not only a place where a Negro may get inspiration, by seeing what other members of his race have accomplished, but a place, also, where he has an opportunity to learn some of the fundamental duties and responsibilites of social and civic life.

Negroes have here, for example, an opportunity, which they do not have to the same degree elsewhere, either in the North or in the South, of entering simply and naturally into all the phases and problems of community life. They are the farmers, the business men, bankers, teachers, preachers. The mayor, the constable, the aldermen, the town marshal, even the station agent, are Negroes.

Black men cleared the land, built the houses, and founded the town. Year by year, as the colony has grown in population, these pioneers have had to face, one after another, all the fundamental problems of civilization. The town is still growing, and as it grows, new and more complicated problems arise. Perhaps the most difficult problem the leaders of the community have to face now is that of founding a school, or a system of schools, in which the younger generation may be able to get some of the kind of knowledge which these pioneers gained in the work of building up and establishing the community.

During the twenty years this town has been in existence it has always had the sympathetic support of people in neighbouring white communities. One reason for this is that the men who have been back of it were born and bred in the Delta, and they know both the land and the people.

Charles Banks was born and raised in Clarksdale, a few miles above Mound Bayou, where he and his brother were for several years engaged in business. It was his good fortune, as has been the case with many other successful Negroes, to come under the influence, when he was a child, of one of the best white families in the city in which he was born. I have several times heard Mr. Banks tell of his early life in Clarksdale and of the warm friends he had made among the best white people in that city.

It happened that his mother was cook for a prominent white family in Clarksdale. In this way he became in a sort of a way attached to the family. It was through the influence of this family, if I remember rightly, that he was sent to Rust University, at Holly Springs, to get his education.

In 1900 Mr. Banks, because of his wide knowledge of local conditions in that part of the country, was appointed supervisor of the census for the Third district of Mississippi. In speaking to me of this matter Mr. Banks said that every white man in town endorsed his application for appointment.

Since he has been in Mound Bayou, Mr. Banks has greatly widened his business connections. The Bank of Mound Bayou now counts among its correspondents banks in Vicksburg, Memphis, and Louisville, together with the National Bank of Commerce of St. Louis and the National Reserve Bank of the City of New York. One of the officers of the former institution, Mr. Eugene Snowden, in a recent letter to me, referring to this and another Negro bank, writes: "It has been my pleasure to lend them $30,000 a year and their business has been handled to my entire satisfaction."

Some years ago, in the course of one of my educational campaigns, I visited Mound Bayou, among other places in Mississippi. Among other persons I met the sheriff of Bolivar County, in which Mound Bayou is situated. Without any suggestion or prompting on my part, he told me that Mound Bayou was one of the most orderly—in fact, I believe he said the most orderly—town in the Delta. A few years ago a newspaper man from Memphis visited the town for the purpose of writing an article about it. What he saw there set him to speculating, and among other things he said:

> Will the Negro as a race work out his own salvation along Mound Bayou lines? Who knows? These have worked out for themselves a better local government than any superior people has ever done for them in freedom. But it is a generally accepted principle in political economy that any homogeneous people will in time do this. These people have their local government, but it is in consonance with the county, state, and national governments and international conventions, all in the hands of another race. Could they conduct as successfully a county government in addition to their local government and still under the state and national governments of another race? Enough Negroes of the Mound Bayou type, and guided as they were in the beginning, will be able to do so.

The words I have quoted will, perhaps, illustrate the sort of interest and sympathy which the Mound Bayou experiment arouses in the minds of thoughtful Southerners. Now it is characteristic of Charles Banks that, in all his talks with me, he has never once referred to the work he is doing as a solution of the problem of the Negro race. He has often referred to it, however, as one step in the solution of the problem of the Delta. He recognizes that, behind everything else, is the economic problem.

Aside from the personal and business interest which he has in the growth and progress of Mound Bayou, Mr. Banks sees in it a means of teaching better methods of farming, of improving the home life, of getting into the masses of the people greater sense of the value of law and order.

I have learned much from studying the success of Charles Banks. Before all else he has taught me the value of common-sense in dealing with conditions as they exist in the South. I have learned from him that, in spite of what the Southern white man may say about the Negro in moments of excitement, the sober sentiment of the South is in sympathy with every effort that promises solid and substantial progress to the Negro.

Maj. R. R. Moton, of Hampton Institute, is one of the few black men I know who can trace his ancestry in an unbroken line on both sides back to Africa. I have often heard him tell the story, as he had it from his grandmother, of the way in which his great-grandfather, who was a young African chief, had come down to the coast to sell some captives taken in war and how, after the bargain was completed, he was enticed on board the white man's ship and himself carried away and sold, along with these unfortunate captives, into slavery in America. Major Moton is, like Charles Banks, not only a full-blooded black man, with a big body and broad Negro features, but he is, in his own way, a remarkably handsome man. I do not think any one could look in Major Moton's face without liking him. In the first place, he looks straight at you, out of big friendly eyes, and as he speaks to you an expression of alert and intelligent sympathy constantly flashes and plays across his kindly features.

It has been my privilege to come into contact with many different types of people, but I know few men who are so lovable and, at the same time, so sensible in their nature as Major Moton. He is chock-full of common-sense. Further than that, he is a man who, without obtruding himself and without your understanding how he does it, makes you believe in him from the very first time you see him and from your first contact with him, and, at the same time, makes you love him. He is the kind of man in whose company I always feel like being, never tire of, always want to be around him, or always want to be near him.

One of the continual sources of surprise to people who come for the first time into the Southern States is to hear of the affection with which white men and women speak of the older generation of coloured people with whom they grew up, particularly the old coloured nurses. The lifelong friendships that exist between these old "aunties" and "uncles" and the white children with whom they were raised is something that is hard for strangers to understand.

It is just these qualities of human sympathy and affection that endeared so many of the older generation of Negroes to their masters and mistresses and which seems to have found expression, in a higher form, in Major Moton. Although he has little schooling outside of what he was able to get at Hampton Institute, Major Moton is one of the best-read men and one of the most interesting men to talk with I have ever met. Education has not "spoiled" him, as it seems to have done in the case of some other educated Negroes. It has not embittered or narrowed him in his affections. He has not learned to hate or distrust any class of people, and he is just as ready to assist and show a kindness to a white man as to a black man, to a Southerner as to a Northerner.

My acquaintance with Major Moton began, as I remember, after he had graduated at Hampton Institute and while he was employed there as a teacher. He had at that time the position that I once occupied in charge of the Indian students. Later he was given the very responsible position he now occupies, at the head of the institute battalion, as commandant of cadets, in which he has charge of the discipline of all the students. In this position he has an opportunity to exert a very direct and personal influence upon the members of the student body and, what is especially important, to prepare them to meet the peculiar difficulties that await them when they go out in the world to begin life for themselves.

It has always seemed to me very fortunate that Hampton Institute should have had in the position which Major Moton occupies a man of such kindly good humour, thorough self-control, and sympathetic disposition.

Major Moton knows by intuition Northern white people and Southern white people. I have often heard the remark made that the Southern white man knows more about the Negro in the South than anybody else. I will not stop here to debate that question, but I will add that coloured men like Major Moton know more about the Southern white man than anybody else on earth.

At the Hampton Institute, for example, they have white teachers and coloured teachers; they have Southern white people and Northern white people; besides, they have coloured students and Indian students. Major Moton knows how to keep his hands on all of these different elements, to see to it that friction is kept down and that each works in harmony with the other. It is a difficult job, but Major Moton knows how to negotiate it.

This thorough understanding of both races which Major Moton possesses has enabled him to give his students just the sort of practical and helpful advice and counsel that no white man who has not himself faced the peculiar conditions of the Negro could be able to give.

I think it would do any one good to attend one of Major Moton's Sunday-school classes when he is explaining to his students, in the very practical way which he knows how to use, the mistake of students allowing themselves to

RUFUS HERRON OF CAMP HILL, ALA.

"If there is a white man, North or South, that has more love for his community or his country than Rufus Herron, it has not been my good fortune to meet him."

be embittered by injustice or degraded by calumny and abuse with which every coloured man must expect to meet at one time or another. Very likely he will follow up what he has to say on this subject by some very apt illustration from his own experience or from that of some of his acquaintances which will show how much easier and simpler it is to meet prejudice with sympathy and understanding than with hatred; to remember that the man who abuses you because of your race probably hasn't the slightest knowledge of you personally, and, nine times out of ten, if you simply refuse to feel injured by what he says, will feel ashamed of himself later.

I think one of the greatest difficulties which a Negro has to meet is in travelling about the country on the railway trains. For example, it is frequently dif-

MAJOR ROBERT RUSSA MOTON

"It has been through contact with men like Major Moton that I have received a kind of education no books could impart."

PROFESSOR GEORGE WASHINGTON CARVER

"One of the most thoroughly scientific men of the Negro race"

ficult for a coloured man to get anything to eat while he is travelling in the South, because, on the train and at the lunch counters along the route, there is often no provision for coloured people. If a coloured man goes to the lunch counter where the white people are served he is very likely, no matter who he may be, to find himself roughly ordered to go around to the kitchen, and even there no provision has been made for him.

Time and again I have seen Major Moton meet this situation, and others like it, by going up directly to the man in charge and telling him what he wanted. More than likely the first thing he received was a volley of abuse. That never discouraged Major Moton. He would not allow himself to be disturbed nor dismissed, but simply insisted, politely and good-naturedly, that he knew the custom, but that he was hungry and wanted something

BISHOP GEORGE W. CLINTON

"He is the kind of man who wins everywhere confidence and respect."

to eat. Somehow, without any loss of dignity, he not only invariably got what he wanted, but after making the man he was dealing with ashamed of himself, he usually made him his friend and left him with a higher opinion of the Negro race as a whole.

I have seen Major Moton in a good many trying situations in which an ordinary man would have lost his head, but I have never seen him when he seemed to feel the least degraded or humiliated. I have learned from Major Moton that one need not belong to a superior race to be a gentleman.

It has been through contact with men like Major Moton—clean, wholesome, high-souled gentlemen under black skins—that I have received a kind of education no books could impart. Whatever disadvantages one may suffer from being a part of what is called an "inferior race," a member of such a race has the advantage of not feeling compelled to go through the world, as some members of other races do, proclaiming their superiority from the house tops. There are some people in this world who would feel lonesome, and they are not all of them white people either, if they did not have some one to whom they could claim superiority.

One of the most distinguished black men of my race is George W. Clinton, of Charlotte, N.C., bishop of the A. M. E. Zion Church. Bishop Clinton was born a slave fifty years ago in South Carolina. He was one of the few young coloured men who, during the Reconstruction days, had an opportunity to attend the University of South Carolina. He prides himself on the fact that he was a member of that famous class of 1874 which furnished one Negro congressman, two United States ministers to Liberia—the most recent of whom is Dr. W. D. Crum—five doctors, seven preachers, and several business men who have made good in after life. Among others was W. McKinlay, the present collector of customs for the port of Georgetown, D.C.

Bishop Clinton has done a great service to the denomination to which he belongs and his years of service have brought him many honours and distinctions. He founded the *African Methodist Episcopal Zion Quarterly Review* and edited, for a time, another publication of the African Methodist Episcopal Zion denomination. He has represented his church in ecumenical conferences at home and abroad, is a trustee of Livingstone College, chairman of the publishing board, has served as a member of the international convention of arbitration and is vice-president of the international Sunday-school union.

Bishop Clinton is a man of a very different type from the other men of pure African blood I have mentioned. Although he says he is fifty years of age, he is in appearance and manner the youngest man in the group. An erect, commanding figure, with a high, broad forehead, rather refined features and fresh, frank, almost boyish manner, he is the kind of man who everywhere wins confidence and respect.

Although Bishop Clinton is by profession a minister, and has been all his life in the service of the Church, he is of all the men I have named the most aggressive in his manner and the most soldierly in his bearing.

Knowing that his profession compelled him to travel about a great deal in all parts of the country, I asked him how a man of his temperament managed to get about without getting into trouble.

"I have had some trouble but not much," he said, "and I have learned that the easiest way to get along everywhere is to be a gentleman. It is simple, convenient, and practicable.

"The only time I ever came near having any serious

trouble," continued Bishop Clinton, "was years ago when I was in politics." And then he went on to relate the following incident: It seems that at this time the Negroes at the bishop's home in Lancaster, S.C., were still active in politics. There was an attempt at one time to get some of the better class of Negroes to unite with some of the Democrats in order to elect a prohibition ticket. The fusion ticket, with two Negroes and four white men as candidates, was put in the field and elected. It turned out, however, that a good many white people cut the Negroes on the ticket and, at the same time, a good many Negroes cut the whites, so that there was some bad blood on both sides. A man who was the editor of the local paper at that time had accused young Clinton of having advised the Negroes to cut the fusion ticket.

"As I knew him well," said the bishop, "I went up to his office to explain. Some rather foolish remark I made irritated the editor and he jumped up and came toward me with a knife in his hands."

The bishop added that he didn't think the man really meant anything "because my mother used to cook in his family" and they had known each other since they were boys, so he simply took hold of his wrists and held them. The bishop is a big, stalwart, athletic man with hands that grip like a vise. He talked very quietly and they settled the matter between them.

Bishop Clinton has told me that he has made many life-long friends among the white people of South Carolina, but this was the only time that he ever had anything like serious trouble with a white man.

I first made the acquaintance of Bishop Clinton when he came to Tuskegee in 1893 as representative of the African Methodist Episcopal Zion Church, at the dedication of the Phelps Hall Bible training school. The next year he came to

Tuskegee as one of the lecturers in that school and he has spent some time at Tuskegee every year since then, assisting in the work of that institution.

Bishop Clinton has been of great assistance to us, not only in our work at Tuskegee, but in the larger work we have been trying to do in arousing interest throughout the country in Negro public schools. He organized and conducted through North Carolina in 1910 what I think was the most successful educational campaign I have yet been able to make in any of the Southern States.

Although he is an aggressive churchman, Bishop Clinton has found time to interest himself in everything that concerns the welfare of the Negro race. He is as interested in the business and economic as he is in the intellectual advancement of the race.

One of the most gifted men of the Negro race whom I ever happened to meet is George W. Carver, Professor Carver, as he is called at Tuskegee, where he has for many years been connected with the scientific and experimental work in agriculture carried on in connection with the Tuskegee Institute. I first met Mr. Carver about 1895 or 1896 when he was a student at the State Agricultural College at Ames, Ia. I had heard of him before that time through Hon. James Wilson, now secretary of agriculture, who was for some time one of Mr. Carver's teachers. It was about this time that an attempt was made to put our work in agriculture on a scientific basis, and Mr. Carver was induced to come to Tuskegee to take charge of that work and of the state experiment station that had been established in connection with it. He has been doing valuable work in that department ever since and, as a result of his work in breeding cotton and of the bulletins be has prepared on experiments in building up wornout soils, he has become widely known to both coloured and white farmers throughout the South.

When some years ago the state secretary of agriculture called a meeting at Montgomery of the leading teachers of the state, Professor Carver was the only coloured man invited to that meeting. He was at that time invited to deliver an address to the convention and for an hour was questioned on the interesting work he was doing at the experiment station.

Professor Carver, like the other men I have mentioned, is of unmixed African blood, and is one of the most thoroughly scientific men of the Negro race with whom I am acquainted. Whenever any one who takes a scientific interest in cotton growing, or in the natural history of this part of the world, comes to visit Tuskegee, he invariably seeks out and consults Professor Carver. A few years ago the colonial secretary of the German empire, accompanied by one of the cotton experts of his department, travelling through the South in a private car, paid a visit of several days to Tuskegee largely to study, in connection with the other work of the school, the cotton-growing experiments that Professor Carver has been carrying on for some years.

In his book, "The Negro in the New World," Sir Harry Johnston, who has himself been much interested in the study of plant life in different parts of the world, says: "Professor Carver, who teaches scientific agriculture, botany, agricultural chemistry, etc., at Tuskegee, is, as regards complexion and features, an absolute Negro; but in the cut of his clothes, the accent of his speech, the soundness of his science, he might be professor of botany, not at Tuskegee, but at Oxford or Cambridge. Any European botanist of distinction, after ten minutes' conversation with this man, instinctively would treat him as a man on a level with himself."

What makes all that Professor Carver has accomplished the more remarkable is the fact that he was born in slavery and has had relatively few opportunities for study, compared with those which a white man who makes himself a scholar in any particular branch of science invariably has.

Professor Carver knows but little of his parentage. He was born on the plantation of a Mr. Carver in Missouri some time during the war.

It was a time when it was becoming very uncomfortable to hold slaves in Missouri and so he and his mother were sent south into Arkansas. After the war Mr. Carver, the master, sent south to inquire what had become of his former slaves. He learned that they had all disappeared with the exception of a child, two or three years old, by the name of George, who was near dead with the whooping-cough and of so little value that the people in Arkansas said they would be very glad to get rid of him.

George was brought home, but he proved to be such a weak and sickly little creature that no attempt was made to put him to work and he was allowed to grow up among chickens and other animals around the servants' quarters, getting his living as best he could.

The little black boy lived, however, and he used his freedom to wander about in the woods, where he soon got on very good terms with all the insects and animals in the forest and gained an intimate and, I might almost say personal, acquaintance with all the plants and the flowers.

As he grew older he began to show unusual aptitude in two directions: He attracted attention, in the first place, by his peculiar knack and skill in all sorts of household work. He learned to cook, to knit and crochet, and he had a peculiar and delicate sense for colour. He learned to draw and, at the present time, he devotes a large part of his leisure to making the most beautiful and accurate drawings of different flowers and forms of plant life in which he is interested.

In the second place, he showed a remarkable natural aptitude and intelligence in dealing with plants. He would spend hours, for example, gathering all the most rare and curious flowers that were to be found in the woods and fields. One day some one discovered that he had established out in the brush a little botanical garden, where he had gathered all sorts of curious plants and where he soon became so expert in making all sorts of things grow, and showed such skill in caring for and protecting plants from all sorts of insects and diseases that he got the name of "the plant doctor."

Another direction in which he showed unusual natural talent was in music. While he was still a child he became famous among the coloured people as a singer. After he was old enough to take care of himself he spent some years wandering about. When he got the opportunity he worked in greenhouses. At one time he ran a laundry; at another time he worked as a cook in a hotel. His natural taste and talent for music and painting, and, in fact, almost every form of art, finally attracted the attention of friends, through whom he secured a position as church organist.

During all this time young Carver was learning wherever he was able. He learned from books when he could get them; learned from experience always; and made friends wherever he went. At last he found an opportunity to take charge of the greenhouses of the horticultural department of the Iowa Agricultural College at Ames. He remained there until he was graduated, when he was made assistant botanist. He took advantage of his opportunities there to continue his studies and finally took a diploma as a postgraduate student, the first diploma of that sort that had been given at Ames.

While he was at the agricultural college in Iowa he took part with the rest of the students in all the activities of college life. He was lieutenant, for example, in the college battalion which escorted Governor Boies to the World's Fair at Chicago. He began to read papers and deliver lectures at the horticultural conventions in all parts of the state. But, in spite of his success in the North, among the people of another race, Mr. Carver was anxious to come South and do something for his own race. So it was that he gladly accepted an invitation to come to Tuskegee and take charge of the scientific and experimental work connected with our department of agriculture.

Although Professor Carver impresses every one who meets him with the extent of his knowledge in the matter of plant life, he is quite the most modest man I have ever met. In fact, he is almost timid. He dresses in the plainest and simplest manner possible; the only thing that he allows in the way of decoration is a flower in his button-hole. It is a rare thing to see Professor Carver any time during the year without some sort of flower on the lapel of his coat and he is particularly proud when he has found somewhere in the woods some especially rare specimen of a flower to show to his friends.

I asked Professor Carver at one time how it was, since he was so timid, that he managed to have made the acquaintance of so many of the best white as well as coloured people in our part of the country. He said that as soon as people found out that he knew something about plants that was valuable he discovered they were very willing and eager to talk with him.

"But you must have some way of advertising," I said jestingly; "how do all these people find out that you know about plants?"

"Well, it is this way," he said. "Shortly after I came here I was going along the woods one day with my botany can under my arm. I was looking for plant diseases and for insect enemies. A lady saw what she probably thought was a harmless old coloured man, with a strange looking box under his arm, and she stopped me and asked if I was a peddler. I told her what I was doing. She seemed delighted and asked me to come and see her roses, which were badly diseased. I showed her just what to do for them—in fact, sat down and wrote it out for her.

"In this," he continued, "and several other ways it became noised abroad that there was a man at the school who knew about plants. People began calling upon me for information and advice."

I myself recall that several years ago a dispute arose down town about the name of a plant. No one knew what it was. Finally one gentleman spoke up and said that they had a man out at the normal school by the name of Carver who could name any plant, tree, bird, stone, etc., in the world, and if he did not know there was no use to look farther. A man was put on a horse and the plant brought to Professor Carver at the Institute. He named it and sent him back. Since then Professor Carver's laboratory has never been free from specimens of some kind.

I have always said that the best means which the Negro has for destroying race prejudice is to make himself a useful and, if possible, an indispensable member of the community in which he lives. Every man and every community is bound to respect the man or woman who has some form of superior knowledge or ability, no matter in what direction it is. I do not know of a better, illustration of this than may be found in the case of Professor Carver. Without any disposition to push himself forward into any position in which he is not wanted, he has been able, because of his special knowledge and ability, to make friends with all classes of people, white as well as black, throughout the South. He is constantly receiving inquiries in regard to his work from all parts of the world, and his experiments in breeding new varieties of cotton have aroused the greatest interest among those cotton planters who are interested in the scientific investigation of cotton growing.

There are few coloured men in the South today who are better or more widely known than Dr. Charles T. Walker, pastor of the Tabernacle Baptist Church of Augusta, Ga. President William H. Taft, referring to Doctor Walker, said that he was the most eloquent man he had ever listened to. For myself I do not know of any man, white or black, who is a more fascinating speaker either in private conversation or on the public platform.

Doctor Walker's speeches, like his conversation, have the charm of a natural-born talker, a man who loves men, and has the art of expressing himself simply, easily, and fluently, in a way to interest and touch them.

On the streets of Augusta, his home, it is no uncommon thing to see Doctor Walker—after the familiar and easy manner of Southern people—stand for hours on a street corner or in front of a grocery store, surrounded by a crowd who have gathered for no other purpose than to hear what he will say. It is said that he knows more than half of the fifteen thousand coloured people of Augusta by name, and when he meets any of them in the street he is disposed to stop, in his friendly and familiar way, in order to inquire about the other members of the family. He wants to know how each is getting on and what has happened to any one of them since he saw them last.

If one of these acquaintances succeeds in detaining him,

he will, very likely, find himself surrounded by other friends and acquaintances and, when once he is fairly launched on one of the quaintly humorous accounts of his adventures in some of the various parts of the world he has visited, or is discussing, in his vivid and epigrammatic way, some public question, business in that part of the town stops for a time.

Doctor Walker is a great story teller. He has a great fund of anecdotes and a wonderful art in using them to emphasize a point in argument or to enforce a remark. I recall that the last time he was at Tuskegee, attending the Negro conference, he told us what he was trying to do at the school established by the Walker Baptist Association at Augusta for the farmers in his neighbourhood. From that he launched off into some remarks upon the coloured farmer, his opportunities, and his progress. He said Senator Tillman had once complained that the coloured farmer wasn't as ignorant as he pretended to be, and then he told this story: He said that an old coloured farmer in his part of the country had rented some land of a white man on what is popularly known as "fourths." By the term of the contract the white man was to get one fourth of the crop for the use of the land.

When it came time to divide the crop, however, it turned out that there were just three wagon loads of cotton and this the old farmer hauled to his own barn.

Of course the landlord protested. He said: "Look here, Uncle Joe, didn't you promise me a fourth of that cotton for my share?"

"Yes, cap'n," was the reply, "Dat's so. I'se mighty sorry, but dere wasn't no fort'."

"How is that?" inquired the landlord.

"There wasn't no fort' 'cause dere was just three wagon loads, and dere wasn't no fort' dere."

Doctor Walker is not only a fascinating conversation-

A MEETING OF THE NEGRO MINISTERS OF MACON COUNTY, ALABAMA

alist, a warm-hearted friend, but he is, also, a wonderfully successful preacher. During the time when he was in New York, as pastor of the Mt. Olivet Baptist Church, his sermons and his wonderful success as an evangelist were frequently reported in the New York papers.

Doctor Walker is not only an extraordinary pulpit orator, but he is a man of remarkably good sense. I recall some instances in particular in which he showed this quality in a very conspicuous way. The first was at a meeting of the National Convention of Negro Baptists at St. Louis in 1886. At this meeting some one delivered an address on the subject, "Southern Ostracism," in which he abused the Southern white Baptists, referring to them as mere figureheads, who believe "there were separate heavens for white and coloured people."

Later, in the session Doctor Walker found an opportunity to reply to these remarks, pointing out that a few months before the Southern Baptist Convention had passed a resolution to expend $10,000 in mission work among the coloured Baptists of the South. He formulated his protest against the remarks made by the speaker of the previous day in a resolution which was passed by the convention.

His speech and the resolution were published in many of the Southern newspapers and denominational organs and did much to change the currents of popular feeling at that time and bring about a better understanding between the races.

Dr. Charles T. Walker was born at the little town of Hepzibah, Richmond County, Ga., about sixteen miles south of his present home, Augusta. His father, who was his master's coachman, was also deacon in the little church organized by the slaves in 1848, of which his uncle was pastor. Doctor Walker comes of a race of preachers. The Walker Baptist Association is named after one of his uncles, Rev. Joseph T. Walker, whose freedom was purchased by the members of his congregation who were themselves slaves. In 1880, upon a resolution of Doctor Walker, this same Walker Association passed a resolution to establish a normal school for coloured children, known as the Walker Baptist Institute. This school has from the first been supported by the constant and unremitting efforts of Doctor Walker.

Meanwhile he has been interested in other good works. He assisted in establishing the Augusta *Sentinel*, and in 1891, while he was travelling in the Holy Land, his accounts of his travels did much to brighten its pages and increase its circulation.

In 1893 he was one of a number of other coloured people to establish a Negro state fair at Augusta, which has continued successfully ever since. Another of his enterprises started and carried on in connection with his church is the Tabernacle Old Folks' Home. He has taken a prominent part in all the religious and educational work of the state and has even dipped, to some extent, into politics, having been at one time a member of the Republican state executive committee.

Aside from these manifold activities, and beyond all he has done in other directions, Doctor Walker has been a man who has constantly sought to take life as he found it and make the most of the opportunities that he saw about him for himself and his people. He has not been an agitator and has done more than any other man I know to bring about peace and good-will between the two sections of the country and the races. It is largely due to his influence that in Augusta, Ga., the black man and the white man live more happily and comfortably than they do in almost any other city in the United States.

The motto of Doctor Walker's life I can state in his own words. "I am determined," he has said, "never to be guilty of ingratitude; never to desert a friend; and never to strike back at an enemy."

It is because of such men as Doctor Walker and many others like him that I have learned not only to respect but to take pride in the race to which I belong.

In seeking to answer the question as to the relative value of the man of pure African extraction and the man of mixed blood I have referred to five men who have gained some distinction in very different walks of life. There are hundreds of others I could name, who, though not so conspicuous nor so well known, are performing in their humble way valuable service for their race and country. I might also mention here the fact that at Tuskegee, during an experience of thirty years, we have found that, although perhaps a majority of our students are not of pure black blood, still the highest honours in our graduating class, namely, that of valedictorian, which is given to students who have attained the highest scholarship during the whole course of their studies, has been about equally divided between students of mixed and pure blood.

For my own part, however, it seems to me a rather unprofitable discussion that seeks to determine in advance the possibilities of any individual or any race or class of individuals. In the first place, races, like individuals, have different qualities and different capacities for service and, that being the case, it is the part of wisdom to give every individual the opportunities for growth and development which will fit him for the greatest usefulness.

When any individual and any race is allowed to find that place, freely and without compulsion, they will not only be happy and contented in themselves, but will fall naturally into the happiest possible relations with all other members of the community.

In the second place, it should be remembered that human life and human society are so complicated that no one can determine what latent possibilities any individual or any race may possess. It is only through education, and through struggle and experiment in all the different activities and relations of life, that it is possible for a race or an individual to find the place in the common life in which they can be of the greatest value to themselves and the rest of the world.

To assume anything else is to deny the value of the free institutions under which we live and of all the centuries of struggle and effort it has cost to bring them into existence.

X

MEETING HIGH AND LOW IN EUROPE

I HAVE gotten an education by meeting all classes of people in the United States. I have been fortunate in getting much education by coming into contact with different classes of people in Europe.

In the course of my journey across Europe I visited, in the fall of 1910, the ancient city of Cracow, the former capital of Poland. It was evening when we reached our destination, and, as we had been travelling all day without sighting an American or any one who spoke English, I began to feel more at sea than I had ever felt, before in my life. I was a little surprised, therefore, as I was getting out of the omnibus, to hear some one say in an unmistakable American accent: "Excuse me, but isn't this Booker T. Washington?"

I replied that it was, and added that I was very glad to hear that kind of a voice in this remote corner of Europe. In a few minutes I was exchanging notes with a man who once lived, he said, in the same part of the country I came from, in West Virginia. He had come originally from Poland and was, I suspect, a Polish Jew, one of that large number of returned immigrants whom one meets in every part of Eastern and Southern Europe.

The next day I met a very intelligent American lady, though of Polish origin, who turned out to be the wife of the Polish count who was the owner and proprietor of the hotel. It was this lady who advised me to go and visit, while I was in Cracow, the tomb of the Polish patriot, Kosciuszko, whose name I had learned in school as one of those revolutionary heroes who, when there was no longer any hope of liberty for their own people in the old world, had crossed the seas to help establish it in the new.

I knew from my school history what Kosciuszko had done for America in its early struggle for independence. I did not know, however, until my attention was called to it in Cracow, what Kosciuszko had done for the freedom and education of my own people.

After his second visit to this country in 1797 Kosciuszko, I learned, made a will in which he bequeathed part of his property in this country in trust to Thomas Jefferson to be used for the purpose of purchasing the freedom of Negro slaves and giving them instruction in the trades and otherwise.

Seven years after his death a school of Negroes, known as the Kosciuszko school, was established in Newark, N.J. The sum left for the benefit of this school amounted to thirteen thousand dollars.

The Polish patriot is buried in the cathedral at Cracow, which is the Westminster Abbey of Poland, and is filled with memorials of the honoured names of that country. Kosciuszko lies in a vault beneath the marble floor of the cathedral. As I looked upon his tomb I thought how small the world is after all, and how curiously interwoven are the interests that bind people together. Here I was in this strange land, farther from my home than I had ever expected to be in my life, and yet I was paying my respects to a man to whom the members of my race owed one of the first permanent schools for them in the United States.

When I visited the tomb of Kosciuszko I placed a rose on it in the name of my race.

A few days later I took a day's journey by train and wagon into a remote part of the country districts of Poland in order to see something of the more primitive peasant life of that region. Away up in the mountains we stopped at a little group of thatched-roof cottages. As I wanted to see what their homes looked like inside, I knocked at the door of one of them and made some inquiry or other in English, not expecting to get a reply that I could understand. I was surprised to hear a man answer me in fairly good English. He told me that he had lived for a long time in Detroit, Mich. My companion, Dr. Robert E. Park, who had also lived in that city, was soon talking familiarly with him about a famous rebel priest, Kolisinski, who had been a leader of the Polish colony in that city.

A week before that I had visited, in the wildest part of Sicily, the sulphur mines of Campo Franco. In the deepest part of these mines I discovered a man who had been a miner in West Virginia, in the same region in which, years before, I had myself learned to mine coal.

These incidents were characteristic of a kind of experience I had everywhere in Europe. In the most remote parts of the country, where I expected to meet people who had, perhaps, never heard of America, I found people who not only spoke my own language, but welcomed me almost as a fellow countryman. All this led me to realize, as I had not been able to do before, the close and intimate way in which the life, the problems, and the people of Europe were touching and influencing America. But it led me also to notice and study the curious and to me surprising reflex influence of America on Europe.

I have made in all three visits to Europe. On my first visit, a number of years ago, I made the journey with no very definite purpose in mind. I kept in the main line of travel and saw what I may call the polite and official side of life in England and some portions of the continent. In London, for example, I was entertained by the American ambassador, Hon. Joseph H. Choate, had the privilege of attending one of the queen's luncheons at Windsor Castle, and made the acquaintance of Hon. James Bryce, the present ambassador to the United States, besides meeting a number of distinguished men whose names were familiar to me in connection with some important phase of the world's work in which they were engaged.

On my last trip I made up my mind to leave, as far as possible, the main highways of travel and see something of the condition of the poorer people, whose lives are neither polite nor picturesque nor pleasant to look at. My purpose in making this trip was to compare, as far as I was able, the condition of the masses of my own people in this country with the masses of the people in Europe, who are in relatively the same situation in political and economic opportunity. I believed that if the black people in America knew something of the burdens and difficulties under which the masses of the people in Europe live and work they would see that their own situation was by no means so hopeless as they have been sometimes taught to believe.

I had another reason for desiring to get acquainted with the situation of people at the bottom in Europe. For a number of years I have been convinced that there is a very intimate relation between the work I have been trying to do at Tuskegee Institute for the masses of the Negroes in the South and the work that was being done for the poorer classes of the people in the different parts of Europe. Different as has been the history of the black man in the South and the white man in Europe, there were, I was convinced, many points in which the life of the one would compare with the life of the other. In the case of the Negro we have a black people struggling up from slavery to freedom: in the other case we have a white man making his way upward through a milder form of subjection and servitude to a position of political and economic independence; and, in each case, the means by which the long journey has been made, in the one instance by a race, in the other by a class, has been, in many respects, the same.

But aside from all that, I was interested in these people for their own sake. An individual or a race that has come up from slavery cannot but feel a peculiar interest and sympathy with any other individual or race that has travelled that same journey or any part of it.

I arrived in London in the late summer. At that time all the polite world, all the distinguished and all the wealthy people, were away in some other part of the world upon their vacations, and the city, as far as these people were concerned, was like a winter residence which had been closed for the summer. But the other six million, whose acquaintance I had determined to make upon this trip, were there.

In one way or another I saw a good deal of the life of the poorer classes, particularly in that vast region inhabited almost wholly by people of the poorer and working classes, which goes under the name of East London. I tramped about at night, visiting the darkest corners of the city I could find. One night I interviewed, on the Thames Embankment, those dreary outcasts of the great city who wander up and down the bank of the river all day and sleep upon the pavement at night. At another time I visited the alehouses and the bar-rooms, where men and women of the poorer classes congregate at night to drink and gossip. I went several times to the police courts in some of the poorer parts of the city, where I had a chance to observe the methods by which the police courts of London deal with the failures and unfortunates of the city who in one way or other fall into the hands of the police.

It had been my plan to give as large a part of my time as possible to getting acquainted with the working classes in the farming regions of Austria, Italy, and Denmark.

To a certain extent the condition of the urban labourers in London connected itself in my mind with the condition of the rural population in other countries I have mentioned, since London represents the largest city population in the world, and England is the country in which the masses of the people have been most completely detached from the land, while Austria, Italy, and Denmark are distinctly agricultural countries, and leaving out Russia, represent the parts of Europe where the people, to a greater extent than elsewhere, live close to the soil.

It is impossible for me to describe in detail what I learned in regard to the condition of the masses of the people in the different parts of Europe I visited. As a rule I suppose the man on the soil has always represented the most backward and neglected portion of the population. This class has everywhere, until recent years, had fewer opportunities for education than the similar classes in the cities and, where the people who tilled the soil have not succeeded in getting possession of the soil—as is especially true in certain parts of Austria-Hungary and lower Italy—they have remained in a condition of greater or less subjection to the landowning classes. In lower Italy, where the masses of the farming population have neither land nor schools, they have remained in a position not far removed from slavery. In

Denmark, on the contrary, where the farming class is, for the most part, made up of independent landowners, not only has agriculture been more thoroughly developed and organized than elsewhere, but farmers are a dominating influence in the political life of the country.

In England, which is the home of political liberty, the working classes have all the political privileges of other Englishmen, although the bulk of the land is in the hands of a comparatively few landowners. On the other hand, the majority of the labourers in the cities have not increased their economic independence. In fact, the English city labourer, from all that I could observe, seemed to be in a position of greater dependence upon his employer and upon the capitalist than is true of any other country I visited.

I recall one incident of my stay in London which emphasized this fact in my mind: I noticed one day a man who was standing, with his hands in his pockets, looking vaguely into the street, one of those types of the casual labourer of whom one meets so many examples in London. I asked if work was plentiful about this time of the year.

"No," he replied. "It is hard to get anything to do, so many people are out of town."

This man looked to me like a dock labourer. I met him somewhere, I think, on or near Mile End Road, in the East End, which is in the centre of a district of over a million inhabitants made up entirely of working people. I told him I could not understand how the absence of a few hundred or a few thousand individuals from a great city like London could make much difference to him. "It makes a great difference, sir," he replied. "Everything seems to stop when they go away."

This man was, to be sure, a casual labourer, one who had, perhaps, been crowded out by competition from the

TOMPKINS MEMORIAL HALL, HAMPTON INSTITUTE

In the Tompkins Memorial Hall 1700 students during the school term take their meals three times daily. The building cost approximately $175,000, and is the largest building on the Institute Grounds.

TRADE SCHOOL AT HAMPTON INSTITUTE

regular avenues of employment. But there is an enormous number of these casual labourers in England. They seem to be a product of the system.

A week or ten days later I met at Skibo Castle in the Highlands of Scotland, Lord John Morley, at that time secretary of state for India. During the time that I was there the question of the condition of the labouring classes was several times touched upon in conversation and some reference was made to the condition I have referred to. I recall that Lord Morley listened to the discussion for some time without making any comment. Then he said very positively that, in spite of all that had been said, the English labourer was, in his opinion, in a greatly better position to-day than he had ever been before in his history. I was the more impressed with this statement because it came from a man who has a world-wide reputation as a scholar and a writer, and who is at the same time a member of what is the most democratic government that has ever ruled in England, a government, also, that has sought to do more than any other to improve the living conditions of the labouring classes.

The experience I had among the poorer classes in London helped me to realize, as I had not done before, the opportunity that the Negro, in spite of the discriminations and injustices from which he suffers, has in America to-day, and particularly in the Southern States, where there is still opportunity to get land, to live in God's open country and in contact with simple, natural things, compared with that of the people in the crowded English cities, where hundreds of thousands of them live practically from hand to mouth and where one tenth of the population, according to an investigation some years ago, are living either in poverty or on the edge of destitution.

At the present moment the national government, in

conjunction with the city of London, is spending immense sums of money in laying out parks, in building public baths, model tenements and lodging houses in some of the poorer quarters of the city. Better than all else, they are building out in the suburbs, on some of the vacant land outside the city, beautiful garden cities, rows and rows of model houses, each with its little garden in front of it, and each provided with every convenience that modern invention and science can suggest to make it healthful, convenient, and comfortable. As a result of this improvement, thousands of working people are being removed every year from the dark, gloomy, and unhealthy regions of the overcrowded city to these free, open spaces, where they have an opportunity to get in contact with God's free air and sunlight.

I confess that I marvelled at the time and interest and money that have been expended not only by the government, but by the philanthropic people of London, in attempting to ameliorate and to raise the level of life among the poorer working classes. I am convinced that if one half or one tenth of the money, interest, and sympathy that have been expended for the education and uplifting of the poorer classes in London were spent upon the Negro in the South, the race problem in our country would be practically solved.

After visiting London, I went, as I have said, to Austria and spent some time in the city of Prague, in Bohemia; in Vienna, Austria, and Budapest, Hungary. While there I had opportunity several times to go out into the country districts and see something of the condition of the farm labourers. From there I went to Sicily. I saw something of the condition of the small farmers in the region of Palermo. I visited the sulphur mines at Campo Franco in the mountainous region of the interior. I passed several days at Catania and saw the grape harvest and the men bare-legged treading the wine in the same way I have read in the Bible. From there I returned and passed several days in Austrian Poland and visited the salt mines. I went out into the country districts and saw the condition of the people in the small country towns in the region around Cracow. I crossed the frontier into Russian Poland and visited a Russian village. From, there I went to Copenhagen and gained new acquaintance with the wonderful things that have been accomplished in the way of organizing and developing agricultural life in that little state.

In thinking over all that I saw and learned during my trip abroad, it seemed to me that I could clearly discern, in all those parts of Europe where the people are most backward, the signs of a great, silent revolution. Everywhere, with perhaps the exception of lower Italy and Sicily, I thought I could see that the man at the bottom was making his way upward and, in doing so, was lifting the level of civilization.

Directly and indirectly this revolution has, to a very considerable extent, been brought about through the influence of the United States. For example, one of the results of the opening up of the great grain fields in the central part of the United States was to break up the whole system of agriculture in every part of Europe where the products of American agriculture come in competition with those of Europe. It was this same competition with American agriculture that provoked the immigration from Austria, Hungary, and southern Italy. I found that wherever the condition of farm labour was particularly bad in Southern Europe the emigration from that part of Europe to America was especially large and increasing. On the other hand, in Denmark, where the agricultural crisis had been overcome by more intensive and intelligent methods of farming, emigration to the United States had almost ceased.

A secondary effect has been to bring about a reorganization of agriculture in such a way as to improve the condition of the farmer. In several countries efforts have been made to break up the large estates and increase the number of small landowners. There has been a very general improvement in the character of the rural schools. The states of Europe, having discovered that their rural population is one of the most important of the natural resources, have begun to take practical measures to educate and improve the neglected masses.

To a large extent it seemed to me that the older civilization had been built up on the ignorance and the oppression of the masses of the people who were at the bottom. The welfare of the few was obtained at the expense of the many. On the other hand, at the present time, wherever any of these countries are successful and are making progress, they are seeking to do so, not by oppressing and holding down the masses of the people, but by building them up, making them more intelligent, more independent, better able to think and care for themselves.

It was, first of all, the competition with America which brought this result about. It was, in the second place, the contact of the masses of the people with life in America which has made the change. I met everywhere in Southern Europe, among the labouring classes of the people, those who had been to America and who had returned. Frequently they had returned with money which they had earned at common labour in America, and had bought and improved property. The number of small landowners has increased greatly in Hungary, Poland, and in southern Italy as the result of the emigration to America. These people came back, sometimes with money, but always with new ideas and new ambitions. They refused to work for the same wages that they had previously worked for. The result was that the price of farm labour has greatly increased, both in Italy and in other parts of Southern Europe.

On the other hand, this compelled the greater use of farm machinery, compelled more intensive and rational methods of agriculture. But nowhere did I find, as some people had expected, that this emigration had had a deterrent effect upon the development of the country. For the labouring masses, particularly in the rural parts of Southern Europe, the journey to America has been a sort of higher education; it has taught them not only to work better and more efficiently, but to have confidence in themselves and to hope and believe in a better future for themselves and their children. In this way the silent revolution to which I refer in Europe has come about.

Now if there is any lesson to be drawn from these facts, it seems to me it is this: that more and more, at the present day, education must take the place of force in the affairs of men. The world is changing. The greatest nation to-day is not the nation with the greatest army, not the nation that can destroy the most, but the nation with the most efficient labourers and the most productive machinery; the nation that can produce the most.

But if labour is to be efficient, it must be trained and it must be free. The school teacher to-day is more important to the state than the soldier, and the aim of the highest statesmanship should be the improvement not so much of the army as of the school.

Although I started out on my last visit to Europe with the determination of getting acquainted with the people at the bottom and made that my main business while I was there, I did, incidentally, have opportunity to see something, also, of the people at the top. In fact, some of the pleasantest and most profitable moments I had during my stay in Europe were those spent in conversation with people who were either interested or actively engaged in some kind of public service which connected itself with the work that I have been trying to do for my own people in America.

For example, I made the acquaintance through my friend, Mr. Jacob Riis, of Mr. V. Cavling, the editor of one of the most important papers in Denmark, the *Politiken*. It was largely through him that I was able to see and learn as much as I did, during the short time that I was there, of the life of the country people and of the remarkable schools that have been established for their benefit in the country districts. While I was in Copenhagen I was introduced by the American ambassador, Mr. Maurice F. Egan, to the king and queen of Denmark. I learned to my surprise that their majesties were perfectly familiar with the work that we are doing at Tuskegee and I found them anxious to talk with me about the possibility of a similar work for the Negroes in the Danish West India Islands, where there are about thirty thousand people of African descent. The queen told me that she had read not only my earlier book "Up From Slavery," but the volume I had just completed, "The Story of the Negro." What surprised me most was to find the king and queen of Denmark so much better informed in regard to the actual condition and progress of the Negro in America than so many Americans I have met.

At another time I was the guest of Mr. Andrew Carnegie at his summer home in Scotland. Three of the most interesting and restful days I have ever had were spent at Skibo Castle. Although Skibo is situated in the wildest and most Northern part of Scotland, farther removed from the world, it seemed to me, than any other place I had ever visited, I never felt nearer the centre of things than I did while I was there.

All kinds of people find their way to Skibo Castle, and apparently any one who has something really valuable to contribute to the world's welfare or progress finds a welcome there.

Naturally, among guests of that sort, conversation and discussion took a wide range. For three days I had an opportunity of hearing great world questions discussed familiarly by men who knew them at first hand. At the time that I met Lord John Morley at Skibo Castle he was still secretary of state for India. I had never been able to get any definite conception, from what I had read in the newspapers, of the actual situation as between the two races in India, the English and the native Indians, and I was very glad to hear Lord Morley comment on that puzzling and perplexing problem. What he said about the matter was the more interesting because he was able to draw parallels between racial conditions in the Eastern and the Western world, between the Indians in India and the Negroes in the United States.

After I returned from the south of Europe I made two addresses in London, one under the auspices of the Anti-slavery and Aborigines Protection Society, and the other at the National Liberal Club. At these meetings I had an opportunity to see face to face people who, as missionaries, writers, or government officials, had, both in Africa and at home, laboured for the welfare and the salvation of the members of my race in parts of the world I had never seen.

For example, at the luncheon given me under the auspices of the Anti-slavery and Aborigines Protection Society, Sir T. Folwell Buxton, grandson of the noted abolitionist and statesman who did so much for the abolition of slavery in the British West Indies, was the presiding officer.

It happened that, at this time, the Society of Friends, which has been from the beginning to the present day, both in England and America, the best friend the Negro has ever had, was holding its annual meeting, and many of the members of this sect were present the day I spoke. Among others I remember, who have distinguished themselves by what they have done for the Negro in Africa were Sir Harry H. Johnston, the noted African explorer; Sir Arthur Conan Doyle, Mr. E. D. Morel, and Rev. J. H. Harris, secretary of the Anti-slavery and Aborigines Protection Society, all of whom have had so large a part in the struggle to bring about reform in the Congo Free State.

Among the many pleasant surprises of this luncheon were a large number of letters from distinguished persons who were unable to be present. Among them, I remember, was a very cordial note from the Prime Minister of England, the Rt. Hon. Herbert Henry Asquith, and among others were two from distinguished personal friends which expressed so generous an appreciation of the work I have attempted to do that I am tempted to reproduce them here. These letters were addressed to John H. Harris, secretary of the Anti-Slavery and Aborigines Protection Society, and were as follows:

SKIBO CASTLE,
DORNECH
SUTHERLAND,
SEPT. 19th, 1910.

DEAR MR. HARRIS:

I regret exceedingly to miss any opportunity of doing honor to one of the greatest men living, Booker Washington. Taking into account his start in life, born a slave, and now the acknowledged leader of his people, I do not know a parallel to the ascent he has made. He has marched steadily upward to undisputed leadership, carrying with this the confidence and approval of the white race, and winning the warm friendship of its foremost members—a double triumph.

Booker Washington is to rank with the few immortals as one who has not only shown his people the promised land, but is teaching them to prove themselves worthy of it—a Joshua and Moses combined.

Very truly yours,

(Signed) ANDREW CARNEGIE.

The other letter, from the Archbishop of Canterbury, was as follows:

It is a great disappointment to me that paramount engagements far away from London render it impossible for me to be present at the gathering which is to give greeting and Godspeed to Mr. Booker T. Washington's acquaintance, and I share with all those who know the facts, the appreciation of the services he has rendered and is rendering to the solution of one of the gravest and most perplexing problems of our time. He is a man who, in every sense, deserves well of his contemporaries, and I believe that, when hereafter the story is written of Christian people's endeavor in our day to atone for and to amend the racial wrongdoing of the past, Mr. Booker T. Washington's name will stand in the very forefront of those for whom the world will give thanks.

It was a great pleasure and satisfaction to me to meet and speak to these distinguished people and the many others whom I met while I was in London. What impressed me through it all was the wide outlook which they had upon the world and its problems. Questions which we in America are inclined to look upon as local and peculiar to our own country assume in the eyes of Englishmen whose interests are not confined to any single country or continent the character of world problems. I learned in England to see that the race problem in the United States is, as Mr. Herbert Samuels, the English postmaster-general said, "a problem which faces all countries in which races of a widely divergent type are living side by side."

The success of the Negro in America and the progress which has been made here in the solution of the racial problem gained wider and deeper meaning for me as a result of my visit to Europe.

XI | WHAT I LEARNED ABOUT EDUCATION IN DENMARK

ON THE railway train between Copenhagen, Denmark, and Hamburg, Germany, I fell into conversation with an English traveller who had been in many parts of the world and who, like myself, was returning from a visit of observation and study in Denmark. We exchanged traveller's experiences with each other. I found that he had had opportunity to study conditions in that country a great deal more thoroughly than was true in my case and he gave me much information that I was glad to have about the condition of agriculture and the life of the people.

In return I told him something of the places I had visited before going to Denmark and of the way I had attempted to dig down, here and there in different parts of Europe, beneath the crust and see what was going on in the lower strata of social life. I said to him, finally, that after all I had seen, I had come to the conclusion that the happiest country in Europe, perhaps the happiest country in the world, is Denmark. Then I asked him if he knew any part of the world where the people seemed to come so near to solving all their problems as in Denmark.

He seemed a little startled and a little amused at that way of putting the matter, but, after considering the question, he confessed that he had never visited any other part of the world that seemed to be in a more generally healthy and wholesome condition than this same little country which we were just leaving behind us.

Denmark is not rich in the sense that England and the United States are rich. I do not know what the statisticians say about the matter, but I suppose that in Denmark there are few if any such great fortunes as one finds in England, in the United States, and in many parts of Europe. In fact, there is hardly room enough in this little land for a multi-millionaire to move about in, as it is less than one third the size of the state of Alabama, although it has one third more population.

Denmark is an agricultural country. About two fifths of the whole population are engaged in some form or other of agriculture. The farms in Denmark have been wonderfully prosperous in recent years. I doubt, however, whether as much money has been made or can be made in Denmark as has been made on the farms in the best agricultural districts in America. The soil is not particularly rich. A large section of the country is, or has been until recent years, made up of barren heath like that in northern Scotland. Within the past few years, as a result of one of the most remarkable pieces of agricultural engineering that has ever been attempted, large tracts of this waste have been made over into fruitful farm land.

In spite of disadvantages, however, the country has greatly prospered for a number of years past. People have been coming from all over the world to study Danish agriculture and they have gone away marvelling at the results. I am not going to try to tell in detail what these results were or in what manner they have been obtained. I will merely say that it seems to be generally conceded that, both in the methods of culture and in the marketing of the crops, Denmark has gone farther and made greater progress than any other part of the world. Furthermore, there is no country, I am certain, not even the United States or Canada, where the average farmer stands so high or exercises so large an influence upon political and social life as he does in Denmark at the present time.

"What's back of the Danish farmer?" I said to my English friend. "What is it that has made agriculture in this country?"

"It's the Danish schools," he replied.

I had asked the same question before and received various replies, but they all wound up with a reference to the schools, particularly the country high schools. I had heard much of them in America; I heard of them again in England; for 90 per cent. of Denmark's agricultural exports goes to England.

It was not, however, until I reached Denmark, saw the schools themselves, and talked with some of the teachers—not, in fact, until after I had left Denmark and had an opportunity to look into and study their history and organization—that I began to comprehend the part that the rural high schools were playing in the life of the masses of the Danish people, and to understand the manner in which they had influenced and helped to build up the agriculture of the country.

There are two things about these rural high schools that were of peculiar interest to me: First, they have had their origin in a movement to help the common people, and to lift the level of the masses, particularly in the rural district; second, they have succeeded. I venture to say that in no part of the world is the general average intelligence of the farming class higher than it is in Denmark. I was impressed in my visits to the homes of some of the small farmers by the number of papers and magazines to be found in their homes.

In recent years there has sprung up in many parts of Europe a movement to improve the condition of the working masses through education. Wherever any effort has been made on a large scale to improve agriculture, it has almost invariably taken the form of a school of some sort or other. For example, in Hungary, the state has organized technical education in agriculture on a grand scale. Nowhere in Europe, I learned, has there been such far-reaching effort to improve agriculture through experimental and research stations, agricultural colleges, high schools, and common schools. There is this difference, however: Hungary has tried to improve agriculture by starting at the top, creating a body of teachers and experts who are expected in turn to influence and direct the classes below them. Denmark has begun at the bottom.

One of the principal aims of the Hungarian Government, as appears from a report by the Minister of Agriculture, was "to adapt the education to the needs of the different classes and take care, at the same time, that these different classes did not learn too much, did not learn anything that would unfit them for their station in life."

I notice, for example, that it was necessary to close the agricultural school at Debreczen, which was conducted in connection with an agricultural college at the same place, because, as the report of the Minister of Agriculture states, "the pupils of this school, being in daily contact with the first-year pupils of the college, attempted to imitate their ways, wanted more than was necessary for their social position, and at the same time aimed at a position they were unable to maintain."

All this is in striking contrast to the spirit and method

of the Danish rural high school, which started among the poorest farming class, and has grown, year by year, until it has drawn within its influence nearly all the classes in the rural community. In this school it happens that the daughters of the peasant and of the nobleman sometimes sit together on the same bench, and that the sons of the landlord and of the tenant frequently work and study side by side, sharing the personal friendship of their teacher and not infrequently the hospitality of his home.

The most striking thing about the rural high school in Denmark is that it is neither a technical nor an industrial school and, although it was created primarily for the peasant people, the subject of agriculture is almost never mentioned, at least not with the purpose of giving practical or technical education in that subject.

It may seem strange that, in a school for farmers, nothing should be said about agriculture, and I confess that it took some time for me to see the connection between this sort of school and Denmark's agricultural prosperity. It seemed to me, as I am sure it will seem to most other persons, that the simplest and most direct way to apply education to agriculture was to teach agriculture in the schools.

The real difference between the Hungarian and the Danish methods of dealing with this problem is, however, in the spirit rather than in the form. In Hungary the purpose of the schools seems to be to give each individual such training as it is believed will fit him for the particular occupation which his station in life assigns him, and no more. The government decides. In other words, education is founded on a system of caste. If the man below learns in school to look to the man in station above him, if he begins to dream and hope for something better than the life to which he has been accustomed—then, a social and political principle is violated, and,

BRICKLAYING AT HAMPTON INSTITUTE

BLACKSMITHING AT HAMPTON INSTITUTE

as the Commisioner of Agriculture says, "the government is not deterred from issuing energetic orders."

Of course, the natural result of such measures is to increase the discontent. Just as soon as any class of people feel that privileges granted to others are denied to them, immediately these privileges—whether they be the opportunities for education, or anything else—assume in the eyes of the people to whom they are denied a new importance and value.

The result of this policy is seen in emigration statistics. I doubt, from what I have been able to learn, whether all the efforts made by the Hungarian Government in the way of agricultural instruction have done very much to allay the discontent among the masses of the farming population. Thousands of these Hungarian peasants every year still prefer to try their fortune in America, and the steady exodus of the farming population continues.

The rural high school in Denmark has pursued just the opposite policy. It has steadily sought to stimulate the ambitions and the intellectual life of the peasant people. Instead, however, of compelling the ambitious farmer's boy, who wants to know something about the world, to go to America, to the ordinary college, or to the city, the schools have brought the learning of the colleges and the advantages of the city to the country.

The most interesting and remarkable thing about these high schools is the success that they have had in presenting every subject that an educated man should know about in such a form as will make it intelligible and interesting to country boys and girls who have only had, perhaps, the rudiments of a common school education.

The teachers in these country high schools are genuine scholars. They have to be, for the reason that the greater part of their teaching is in the form of lectures, without textbooks of any kind, and their success depends upon the skill with which they can present their subjects. In order to awaken interest and enthusiasm, they have to go to the sources for their knowledge.

Most of the teachers whom I met could speak two or three languages. I was surprised at the knowledge which every one I met in Denmark, from the King and Queen to the peasants, displayed in American affairs, and the interest they showed in the progress of the Negro and the work we have been doing at Tuskegee. As an illustration of the wide interests which occupy the teachers in these rural schools, I found one of them engaged in translating Prof. William James's book on "Pragmatism" into the Danish language.

I have heard it said repeatedly since I was in Denmark that the Danish people as a whole were better educated and better informed than any other people in Europe. Statistics seem to bear out this statement; for, according to the immigration figures of 1900, although 24.2 per cent. of all persons over fourteen years of age coming into the United States as immigrants could neither read nor write, only .8 per cent. of the immigrants from Scandinavia were illiterate. Of the Germans, among whom I had always supposed education was more widely diffused than elsewhere in Europe, 5.8 per cent. were illiterate.

Before I go farther, perhaps, I ought to give some idea of what these rural high schools look like. One of the most famous of them is situated about an hour's ride from Copenhagen, near the little city of Roskilde. It stands on a piece of rolling ground, overlooking a bay, where the little fisher vessels and small seafaring craft are able to come far inland, almost to the centre of the island. All around are wide stretches of rich farm land, dotted here and there with little country villages.

There is, as I remember, one large building with a wing at either end. In one of these wings the head master of the school lives, and in the other is a gymnasium. In between are the school rooms where the lectures are held. Everything about the school is arranged in a neat and orderly manner— simple, clean, and sweet—and I was especially impressed by the wholesome, homelike atmosphere of the place. Teachers and pupils eat together at the same table and meet together in a social way in the evening. Teachers and students are thus not merely friends; they are in a certain sense comrades.

In the school at Roskilde there are usually about one hundred and fifty students. During the winter term of five months the young men are in school; in the summer the young women take their turn. Pupils pay for board and lodging twenty crowns, a little more than five dollars a month, and for tuition, twenty crowns the first month, fifteen the second, ten the third, five the fourth, and nothing the fifth. These figures are themselves an indication of the thrift as well as the simplicity with which these schools are conducted. Twenty years ago, when they were first started, I was told the pupils used to sleep together, in a great sleeping room on straw mattresses, and eat with wooden spoons out of a common dish, just as the peasant people did at that time. This reminds me that just about this same time, at Tuskegee, pupils were having similar hardships. For one thing, I recall that, in those days, the food for the whole school was cooked in one large iron kettle and that sometimes we had to skip a meal because there wasn't anything to put in the kettle. Since that time conditions have changed, not only in the rural high schools of Denmark, but among the country people. At the present day, if not every peasant cottage, at least every cooperative dairy has its shower-bath. The small farmer, who, a few years ago, looked upon every innovation with mistrust, is likely now to have his own telephone—for Denmark has more telephones to the number of the population than has any other country in Europe—and every country village has its gymnasium and its assembly hall for public lectures.

I have before me, on my desk, a school plan showing the manner in which the day is disposed of. School begins at eight o'clock in the morning and ends at seven o'clock in the evening, with two hours rest at noon. Two thirds of the time of the school is devoted to instruction in the Danish mother-tongue and in history. The rest is given to arithmetic, geography, and the natural sciences.

It is peculiar to these schools that most of the instruction is given in the form of lectures. There are no examinations and few recitations. Not only the natural sciences, but even the higher mathematics, are taught historically, by lectures.

The purpose is not to give the student training in the use of these sciences, but to give him a general insight into the manner in which different problems have arisen and of the way in which the solution of them has widened and increased our knowledge of the world.

In the Danish rural high school, emphasis is put upon the folk-songs, upon Danish history and the old Northern mythology. The purpose is to emphasize, in opposition to the Latin and Greek teaching of the colleges, the value of the history and the culture of the Scandinavian people; and, incidentally, to instil into the minds of the pupils the patriotic conviction that they have a place and mission of their own among the people of the world.

There are several striking things about this system of rural high schools, of which there are now 120 in Denmark. The first thing about them that impressed me was the circumstances in which they had their origin. In the beginning the rural high schools were a private undertaking, as indeed they are still, although they get a certain amount of support from the State. The whole scheme was worked out by a few courageous individuals, who were sometimes opposed, but frequently assisted by the Government. The point which I wish to emphasize is that they did not spring into existence all at once, but that they grew up slowly and are still growing. It took long years of struggles to formulate and popularize the plans and methods which are now in use in these schools. In this work the leading figure was a Lutheran bishop, Nicolai Frederick Severen Grundvig, who is often referred to as the Luther of Denmark. The rural school movement grew out of a non-sectarian religious movement and was, in fact, an attempt to revive the spiritual life of the masses of the people.

Rural high schools were established as early as 1844, but it was not until twenty years later, when Denmark, as a result of her disastrous war with Prussia, had lost one third of her richest territory, that the rural high school movement began to gain ground. It was at that time, when affairs were at their lowest ebb in Denmark, that Grundvig began preaching to the Danish people the gospel that what had been lost without, must be regained within; and that what had been lost in battle must be gained in peaceful development of the national resources.

Bishop Grundvig saw that the greatest national resource of Denmark, as it is of any country, was its common people. The schools he started and the methods of education he planned were adapted to the needs of the masses. They were an attempt to popularize learning, put it in simple language, rob it of its mystery and make it the common property of the common people.

Another thing peculiar about these schools is that they

were not for children, but for older students. Eighty per cent. of the students in the rural high schools are from eighteen to twenty-five years of age; 12 per cent. are more than twenty-five years of age and only 8 per cent. are under eighteen. These schools, are, in fact, farmers' colleges. They presuppose the education of the common school. The farmer's son and the farmer's daughter, before they enter the rural high school, have had the training in the public schools and have had practical schooling in the work of the farm and the home. At just about the age when a boy or a girl begins to think about leaving home and of striking out in the world for himself; just at the age when there, comes, if ever, to a youth the desire to know something about the larger world and about all the mysteries and secrets that are buried away in books or handed down as traditions in the schools—just at this time the boys and girls are sent away to spend two seasons or more in a rural high school. As a rule they go, not to the school in their neighbourhood but to some other part of the country. There they make the acquaintance of other young men and women who, like themselves, have come directly from the farms, and this intercourse and acquaintance helps to give them a sense of common interest and to build up what the socialists call a "class consciousness." All of this experience becomes important a little later in the building up of the cooperative societies, cooperative dairies, cooperative slaughter houses, societies for the production and sale of eggs, for cattle raising and for other purposes.

The present organization of agriculture in Denmark is indirectly but still very largely due to the influence of the rural school.

The rural high school came into existence, as I have said, as the result of a religious rather than of a merely social or economic movement. Different in methods and in outward form as these high schools are from the industrial schools for the Negro in America, they have this in common, that they are non-sectarian, but in the broadest, deepest sense of that word, religious. They seek, not merely to broaden the minds, but to raise and strengthen the moral life of masses of the people. This peculiar character of the Danish rural high school was defined to me in one word by a gentleman I met in Denmark. He called them "inspirational."

It is said of Grundvig that he was one of those who did not look for salvation merely in political freedom. In spite of this fact, the rural high schools have had a large influence upon politics in Denmark. It is due to them, although they have carefully abstained from any kind of political agitation, that Denmark, under the influence of its "Peasant Ministry," has become the most democratic country in Europe. It is certainly a striking illustration of the result of this education that what, a comparatively few years ago, was the lowest and the most oppressed class in Denmark, namely the small farmer, has become the controlling power in the State, as seems to be the case at the present time.

I have gone to some length to describe the plans and general character of the rural high schools because they are the earliest, the most peculiar and unusual feature in Danish rural life and education, and because, although conducted in the same spirit, they are different in form and methods from the industrial schools with which I have been mainly interested during the greater part of my life.

The high schools, however, are only one part of the Danish system of rural schools. In recent years there has grown up side by side with the rural high school another type of school for the technical training in agriculture and in the household arts. For example, not more than half a mile from the rural high school which I visited at Roskilde, there has recently been erected what we in America would call an industrial school, where scientific agriculture, as well as technical training in homekeeping are given. In this school, young men and women get much the same practical training that is given our students at Tuskegee, with the exception that this training is confined to agriculture and housekeeping. Besides, there is, in these agricultural schools, no attempt to give students a general education as is the case with the industrial schools in the South. In fact, schools like Hampton and Tuskegee are trying to do for their students at one and the same time, what is done in Denmark through two distinct types of school.

I found this school, like its neighbour the high school, admirably situated, surrounded by beautiful gardens in which the students raised their own vegetables. In the kitchen, the young women learned to prepare the meals and to set the tables. I was interested to see also that, in the whole organization of the school there was an attempt to preserve the simplicity of country life. In the furniture, for example, there was an attempt to preserve the solid simplicity and quaint artistic shapes with which the wealthier peasants of fifty or a hundred years ago furnished their homes. Dr. Robert E. Park, my companion on my trip through Europe, told me when I visited this school that he found one of the professors at work in the garden wearing the wooden shoes that used to be worn everywhere in the country by the peasant people. This man had travelled widely, had studied in Germany, where he had taken a degree in his particular specialty at one of the agricultural colleges.

Perhaps the most interesting and instructive part of my visit was the time that I spent at what is called a husmand's or cotter's school, located at Ringsted and founded by N. J.

Nielsen-Klodskov in 1902. At this school I saw such an exhibition of vegetables, grains, and especially of apples, as I think I had never seen before, certainly not at any agricultural school.

I wish I had opportunity to describe in detail all that I saw and learned about education and the possibilities of country life in the course of my visit to this interesting school. What impressed me most with regard to it and to the others that I visited, was the way in which the different types of schools in Denmark have succeeded in working into practical harmony with one another; the way also, in which each in its separate way had united with the other to uplift, vivify, and inspire the life and work of the country people.

For example, the school at Ringsted, in addition to the winter course in farming for men and the summer school in household arts for women, offers, just as we do at Tuskegee, a short course to which the older people are invited. The courses are divided between the men and the women, the men's course coming in the winter and the women's course in the summer. During the period of instruction, which lasts eleven days, these older people live in the school, just as the younger students do and gain thus the benefit of an intimate association with each other and with their teachers. To illustrate to what extent this school and the others like it have reached and touched the people, I will quote from a letter written to me by the founder. He says: "The Keorehave Husmandskole (cotter's school) is the first of its kind in Denmark. It is a private undertaking and the buildings erected since 1902 are worth about 400,000 crowns ($100,000). During the seven years in which it has been in operation 631 men and 603 women have had training for six months. In addition 3,205 men and women have attended the eleven-day courses."

In addition to the short courses in agriculture and housekeeping, offered by the school at Ringsted, some of the rural high schools hold, every fall, great public assembles like our Chautauquas, which last from a few days to a week and are attended by men and women of the rural districts. At these meetings there are public lectures on historical, literary and religious subjects. In the evening there are music, singing, and dancing, and other forms of amusement. These annual assemblies, held under the direction of the rural high schools, have largely taken the place of the former annual harvest-home festivals in which there was much eating and drinking, as I understand, but very little that was educational or uplifting. In addition to these yearly meetings, which draw together people from a distance, there are monthly meetings which are held either in the high school buildings, or in the village assembly buildings, or in the halls connected with the village gymnasiums. In the cities these meetings are sometimes held in the "High School Homes" as they are called, which serve the double purpose of places for the meetings of young men's and young women's societies and at the same time as cheap and home-like hotels for the travelling country people.

In this way the rural high schools have extended their influence to every part of the country, making the life on the farm attractive, and enabling Denmark to set before the world an example of what a simple, wholesome, and beautiful country life can be.

No doubt there are in the country life of Denmark, as of other countries, some things that cast a shadow here and there on the bright picture I have drawn. New problems always spring up out of the solution of the old ones. No matter how much has been accomplished those who know conditions best will inevitably feel that their work has just been begun. However that may be, I do not believe there will be found anywhere a better illustration of the possibilities of education than in the results achieved by the rural schools of Denmark.

One of the things that one hears a great deal of talk about in America is the relative value of cultural and vocational education. I do not think that I clearly understood until I went to Denmark what a "cultural" education was. I had gotten the idea, from what I had seen of the so-called "cultural" education in America, that culture was always associated with Greek and Latin, and that people who advocated it believed there was some mysterious, almost magical power which was to be gotten from the study of books, or from the study of something ancient and foreign, far from the common and ordinary experiences of men. I found, in Denmark, schools in which almost no text-books are used, which were more exclusively cultural than any I had ever seen or heard of.

I had gotten the impression that what we ordinarily called culture was something for the few people who are able to go to college, and that it was somehow bottled up and sealed in abstract language and in phrases which it took long years of study to master. I found in Denmark real scholars engaged in teaching ordinary country people, making it their peculiar business to strip the learning of the colleges of all that was technical and abstract and giving it, through the medium of the common speech, to the common people.

Cultural education has usually been associated in my mind with the learning of some foreign language, with learning the history and traditions of some other people. I found in Denmark a kind of education which, although as far as it went touched every subject and every land that it was the business of the educated man to know about, sought especially to inspire an interest and enthusiasm in the art, the traditions, the language, and the history of Denmark and in the people by whom the students were surrounded. I saw that a cultural education could be and should be a kind of education that helps to awaken, enlighten, and inspire interest, enthusiasm, and faith in one's self, in one's race and in mankind; that it need not be, as it sometimes has been in Denmark and elsewhere, a kind of education that robs its pupils of their natural independence, makes them feel that something distant, foreign, and mysterious is better and higher than what is familiar and close at hand.

I have never been especially interested in discussing the question of the particular label that should be attached to any form of education; I have never taken much interest, for example, in discussing whether the form of education which we have been giving our students at Tuskegee was cultural, vocational, or both. I have been only interested in seeing that it was the kind that was needed by the masses of the people we were trying to reach, and that the work was done as well as possible under the circumstances. From what I have learned in Denmark, I have discovered that what has been done, for example, by Dr. R. H. Boyd in teaching the Negro people to buy Negro instead of white dolls for their children, "in order," as Dr. Boyd says, "to teach the children to admire and respect their own type"; that what has been done at Fisk University to inspire in the Negro a love of folksongs; that what has been done at Tuskegee in our annual Negro Conferences, and in our National Business League, to awaken an interest and enthusiasm in the masses of the people for the common life and progress of the race has done more good, and, in the true sense of the word, been more cultural than all the Greek and Latin that have ever been studied by all Negroes in all the colleges in the country.

For culture of this kind spreads over more ground; it touches more people and touches them more deeply. My study of the Danish rural schools has not only taught me what may be done to inspire and foster a national and racial spirit, but it has shown how closely interwoven are the moral and material conditions of the people, so that each man responds to and reflects the progress of every other man in a way to bring about a healthful, wholesome condition of national and racial life.

XII | THE MISTAKES AND THE FUTURE OF NEGRO EDUCATION

D URING the thirty years I have been engaged in Negro education in the South my work has brought me into contact with many different kinds of Negro schools. I have visited these schools in every part of the South and have had an opportunity to study their work and learn something of their difficulties as well as of their successes. During the last five years, for example, I have taken time from my other work to make extended trips of observation through eight different states, looking into the condition of the schools and saying a word, wherever I went, in their interest. I have had opportunities, as I went about, to note not merely the progress that has been made inside the school houses, but to observe, also, the effects which the different types of schools have had upon the homes and in the communities by which they are surrounded.

Considering all that I have seen and learned of Negro education in the way I have described, it has occurred to me that I could not do better in the concluding reminiscences of my own larger education than give some sort of summary statement, not only of what has been accomplished, but what seems to be the present needs and prospects of Negro education in general for the Southern States. In view also of the fact that I have gained the larger part of my own larger education in what I have been able to do for this cause, the statement may not seem out of place here. Let me then, first of all, say that never in the history of the world has a people, coming so lately out of slavery, made such efforts to catch up with and attain the highest and best in the civilization about them; never has such a people made the same amount of progress in the same time as is the case of the Negro people of America.

At the same time, I ought to add, also, that never in the history of the world has there been a more generous effort on the part of one race to help civilize and build up another than has been true of the American white man and the Negro. I say this because it should be remembered that, if the white man in America was responsible for bringing the Negro here and holding him in slavery, the white man in America was equally responsible for giving him his freedom and the opportunities by which he has been able to make the tremendous progress of the last forty-eight years.

In spite of this fact, in looking over and considering conditions of Negro education in the South to-day, not so much with reference to the past as to the future, I am impressed with the imperfect, incomplete, and unsatisfactory condition in which that education now is I fear that there is much misconception, both in the North and in the South, in regard to the actual opportunities for education which the Negro has.

In the first place, in spite of all that has been said about it, the mass of the Negro people has never had, either in the common schools or in the Negro colleges in the South, an education in the same sense as the white people in the

Northern States have had an education. Without going into details, let me give a few facts in regard to the Negro schools of so-called higher learning in the South. There are twenty-five Negro schools which are ordinarily classed as colleges in the South. They have, altogether, property and endowments, according to the report of the United States commissioner of education, of $7,993,028. There are eleven single institutions of higher learning in the Northern States, each of which has property and endowment equal to or greater than all the Negro colleges in the South. There are, for instance, five colleges or universities in the North every one of which has property and endowments amounting to more than $20,000,000; there are three universities which together have property and endowments amounting to nearly $100,000,000.

The combined annual income of twenty-four principal Negro colleges is $1,048,317. There are fifteen white schools that have a yearly income of from one million to five million dollars each. In fact, there is one single institution of learning in the North which, in the year of 1909, had an income, nearly twice as large as the combined income of the one hundred and twenty-three Negro colleges, industrial schools, and other private institutions of learning of which the commissioner of education has any report. These facts indicate, I think, that however numerous the Negro institutions of higher learning may be, the ten million Negroes in the United States are not getting from them, either in quality or in quantity, an education such as they ought to have.

Let me speak, however, of conditions as I have found them in some of the more backward Negro communities. In my own state, for example, there are communities in which Negro teachers are now being paid not more than from fif-

teen dollars to seventeen dollars a month for services covering
a period of three or four months in the year. As I stated in a
recent open letter to the Montgomery *Advertiser*, more money
is paid for Negro convicts than for Negro teachers. About
forty-six dollars a month is now being paid for first-class, able-
bodied Negro convicts, thirty-six dollars for second-class, and
twenty-six dollars for third-class, and this is for twelve months
in the year. This will, perhaps, at least suggest the conditions
that exist in some of the Negro rural schools.

I do not mean to say that conditions are as bad everywhere as these that I refer to. Nevertheless, when one speaks
"of the results of Negro education" it should be remembered that, so far as concerns the masses of the Negro
people, education has never yet been really tried.

One of the troubles with Negro education at the present
time is that there are no definite standards of education
among the different Negro schools. It is not possible to tell,
for instance, from the name of an institution, whether it is
teaching the ordinary common school branches, Greek and
Latin, or carpentry, blacksmithing, and sewing. More than
that, there is no accepted standard as to the methods or efficiency of the teaching in these schools. A student may be getting a mere smattering, not even learning sufficient reading
and writing to be able to read with comfort a book or a
newspaper. He may be getting a very good training in one
subject and almost nothing in some other. A boy entering
such a school does not know what he is going for, and, nine
times out of ten, he will come away without knowing what
he got. In many cases, the diploma that the student carries
home with him at the conclusion of his course is nothing less
than a gold brick. It has made him believe that he has gotten
an education, when he has actually never had an opportunity
to find out what an education is.

I have in mind a young man who came to us from one of those little colleges to which I have referred where he had studied Greek, Latin, German, astronomy, and, among other things, stenography. He found that he could not use his Greek and Latin and that he had not learned enough German to be able to use the language, so he came to us as a stenographer. Unfortunately, he was not much better in stenography and in English than he was in German. After he had failed as a stenographer, he tried several other things, but because he had gone through a college and had a diploma, he could never bring himself to the point of fitting himself to do well any one thing. The consequence was that he went wandering about the country, always dissatisfied and unhappy, never giving satisfaction to himself or to his employers.

Although this young man was not able to write a letter in English without making grammatical errors or errors of some kind or other, the last time I heard of him he was employed as a teacher of business, in fact, he was at the head of the business department in one of the little colleges to which I have referred. He was not able to use his stenography in a well-equipped office, but he was able to teach stenography sufficiently well to meet the demands of the business course as given in the kind of Negro college of which there are, unfortunately, too many in the South.

Now, there was nothing the matter with this young man—excepting his education. He was industrious, ambitious, absolutely trustworthy, and, if he had been able to stick at any one position long enough to learn to do the work required of him well, he would have made, in my opinion, a very valuable man. As it was, his higher education spoiled him. In going through college he had been taught that he was getting an education when, as a matter of fact, he really had no education worth the mention.

One of the mistakes that Negro schools have frequently made has been the effort to cover, in some sort of way, the whole school curriculum from the primary, through the college, taking their students, as a friend of mine once said, "from the cradle to the grave." The result is that many of the Negro colleges have so burdened themselves with the work of an elementary grade that they are actually doing no college work at all, although they still keep up the forms and their students still speak of themselves as "college students."

In this way nearly every little school calling itself a college has attempted to set up a complete school system of its own, reaching from the primary grade up through the university. These schools, having set themselves an impossible task, particularly in view of the small means that they have at their command, it is no wonder that their work is often badly done.

I remember visiting one of these institutions in the backwoods district of one of the Southern States. The school was carried on in an old ramshackle building, which had been erected by the students and the teachers, although it was evident that not one of them had more than the most primitive notion of how to handle a saw or a square.

The wind blew through the building from end to end. Heaps of Bibles, which had been presented to the school by some friends, were piled up on the floor in one corner of the building. The dormitory was in the most disorderly condition one could possibly imagine. Half of the building had been burned away and had never been rebuilt. Broken beds and old mattresses were piled helter-skelter about in the rooms. What showed as well as anything the total incompetency of everybody connected with the school were the futile efforts that had been made to obtain a supply of drinking water. The yard around the school, which they called the "campus," was full of deep and dangerous holes, where some one had attempted at different times to dig a well but failed, because, as was evident enough, he had not the slightest idea of how the work should have been done.

At the time I was there the school was supplied with water from an old swamp in the neighbourhood, but the president of the college explained to me an elaborate plan which he had evolved for creating an artificial lake and this enterprise, he said, had the added advantage of furnishing work for the students.

When I asked this man in regard to his course of study, he handed me a great sheet of paper, about fifteen inches wide and two feet long, filled with statements that he had copied from the curricula of all sorts of different schools, including theological seminaries, universities, and industrial schools. From this sheet, it appeared that he proposed to teach in his school everything from Hebrew to telegraphy. In fact, it would have taken at least two hundred teachers to do all the work that he had laid out.

When I asked him why it was that he did not confine himself within the limits of what the students needed and of what he would be able to teach, he explained to me that he had found that some people wanted one kind of education and some people wanted another. As far as he was concerned, he took a liberal view and was willing to give anybody anything that was wanted. If his students wanted industrial education, theological education, or college education, he proposed to give it to them.

I suggested to him that the plan was liberal enough, but it would be impossible for him to carry it out. "Yes," he replied, "it may be impossible just now, but I believe in aiming high." The pathetic thing about it all was that this man and the people with whom he had surrounded himself were perfectly sincere in what they were trying to do. They simply did not know what an education was or what it was for.

We have in the South, in general, five types of Negro schools. There are (1) the common schools, supported in large part by state funds supplemented in many cases by contributions from the coloured people; (2) academies and so-called colleges, or universities, supported partly by different Negro religious denominations and partly by the contributions of philanthropic persons and organizations; (3) the state normal, mechanical, and agricultural colleges, supported in part by the state and in part by funds provided by the Federal Government; (4) medical schools, which are usually attached to some one or other of the colleges, but really maintain a more or less independent existence; (5) industrial schools, on the model of Hampton and Tuskegee.

Although these schools exist, in many cases, side by side, most of them are attempting to do, more or less, the work of all the others. Because every school is attempting to do the work of every other, the opportunities for coöperation and team work are lost. Instead one finds them frequently quarrelling and competing among themselves both for financial support and for students. The colleges and the academies frequently draw students away from the public schools. The state agricultural schools, supported in part by the National Government, are hardly distinguishable from some of the theological seminaries. Instead of working in coöperation with one another and with the public authorities in building up the public schools, thus bringing the various institutions of learning into some sort of working harmony and system, it not infrequently happens that the different schools are spending time and energy in trying to hamper and injure one another.

We have had some experience at Tuskegee of this lack

of coöperation among the different types of Negro schools. For some years we have employed as teachers a large number of graduates, not only from some of the better Negro colleges in the South, but from some of the best colleges in the North as well. In spite of the fact that Tuskegee offers a larger market for the services of these college graduates than they are able to find elsewhere, I have yet to find a single graduate who has come to us from any of these colleges in the South who has made any study of the aims or purposes of industrial education. And this is true, although some of the colleges claim that a large part of their work consists in preparing teachers for work in industrial schools.

Not only has it been true that graduates of these colleges have had no knowledge or preparation which fitted them for teaching in an industrial school, but in many cases, they have come to us with the most distorted notions of what these industrial schools were seeking to do.

Perhaps the larger proportion of the college graduates go, when they leave college, as teachers into the city or rural schools. Nevertheless, there is the same lack of coöperation between the colleges and the public schools that I have described as existing between the colleges and the industrial schools. It is a rare thing, so far as my experience goes, for students in the Negro colleges to have had an opportunity to make any systematic study of the actual condition and needs of the schools or communities in which they are employed after they graduate. Instead of working out and teaching methods of connecting the school with life, thus making it a centre and a source of inspiration that might gradually transform the communities about them, these colleges have too frequently permitted their graduates to go out with the idea that their diploma was a sort of patent of nobility, and that the possessor of it was a superior being who was making a sacrifice in merely bestowing himself or herself as a teacher upon the communities to which he or she was called.

One of the chief hindrances to the progress of Negro education in the public schools in the South is in my opinion due to the fact that the Negro colleges in which so many of the teachers are prepared have not realized the importance of convincing the Southern white people that education makes the same improvement in the Negro that it does in the white man; makes him so much more useful in his labour, so much better a citizen, and so much more dependable in all the relations of life, that it is worth while to spend the money to give him an education. As long as the masses of the Southern white people remain unconvinced by the results of the education which they see about them that education makes the Negro a better man or woman, so long will the masses of the Negro people who are dependent upon the public schools for their instruction remain to a greater or less extent in ignorance.

Some of the schools of the strictly academic type have declared that their purpose in sticking to the old-fashioned scholastic studies was to make of their students Christian gentlemen. Of course, every man and every woman should be a Christian and, if possible, a gentleman or a lady; but it is not necessary to study Greek or Latin to be a Christian. More than that, a school that is content with merely turning out ladies and gentlemen who are not at the same time something else—who are not lawyers, doctors, business men, bankers, carpenters, farmers, teachers, not even housewives, but merely ladies and gentlemen—such a school is bound, in my estimation, to be more or less of a failure. There is no room in this country, and never has been, for the class of people who are merely gentlemen, and, if I may judge from

COLLIS P. HUNTINGTON MEMORIAL BUILDING

Tuskegee Institute

THE OFFICE BUILDING

In which are located the administrative offices of the school,
the Institute Bank and the Institute Post Office

what I have lately seen abroad, the time is coming when there will be no room in any country for the class of people who are merely gentlemen—for people, in other words, who are not fitted to perform some definite service for the country or the community in which they live.

In the majority of cases I have found that the smaller Negro colleges have been modelled on the schools started in the South by the anti-slavery people from the North directly after the war. Perhaps there were too many institutions started at that time for teaching Greek and Latin, considering that the foundation had not yet been laid in a good common-school system. It should be remembered, however, that the people who started these schools had a somewhat different purpose from that for which schools ordinarily exist to-day. They believed that it was necessary to complete the emancipation of the Negro by demonstrating to the world that the black man was just as able to learn from books as the white man, a thing that had been frequently denied during the long anti-slavery controversy.

I think it is safe to say that that has now been demonstrated. What remains to be shown is that the Negro can go as far as the white man in using his education, of whatever kind it may be, to make himself a more useful and valuable member of society. Especially is it necessary to convince the Southern white man that education, in the case of the coloured man, is a necessary step in the progress and upbuilding, not merely of the Negro, but of the South.

It should be remembered in this connection that there are thousands of white men in the South who are perfectly friendly to the Negro and would like to do something to help him, but who have not yet been convinced that education has actually done the Negro any good. Nothing will change their minds but an opportunity to see results for themselves.

The reason more progress has not been made in this direction is that the schools planted in the South by the Northern white people have remained—not always through their own fault to be sure—in a certain sense, alien institutions. They have not considered, in planning their courses of instruction, the actual needs either of the Negro or of the South. Not infrequently young men and women have gotten so out of touch during the time that they were in these schools with the actual conditions and needs of the Negro and the South that it has taken years before they were able to get back to earth and find places where they would be useful and happy in some form or other of necessary and useful labour.

Sometimes it has happened that Negro college students, as a result of the conditions under which they were taught, have yielded to the temptation to become mere agitators, unwilling and unfit to do any kind of useful or constructive work. Naturally under such conditions as teachers, or in any other capacity, they have not been able to be of much use in winning support in the South for Negro education. Nevertheless it is in the public schools of the South that the masses of the Negro people must get their education, if they are to get any education at all.

I have long been of the opinion that the persons in charge of the Negro colleges do not realize the extent to which it is possible to create in every part of the South a friendly sentiment toward Negro education, provided it can be shown that this education has actually benefited and helped in some practical way the masses of the Negro people with whom the white man in the South comes most in contact. We should not forget that as a rule in the South it is not the educated Negro, but the masses of the people, the farmers, labourers, and servants, with whom the white people come in daily contact.

If the higher education which is given to the few does not in some way directly or indirectly reach and help the masses very little will be done toward making Negro education popular in the South or toward securing from the different states the means to carry it on.

On the other hand, just so soon as the Southern white man can see for himself the effects of Negro education in the better service he receives from the labourer on the farm or in the shop; just so soon as the white merchant finds that education is giving the Negro not only more wants, but more money with which to satisfy these wants, thus making him a better customer; when the white people generally discover that Negro education lessens crime and disease and makes the Negro in every way a better citizen, then the white taxpayer will not look upon the money spent for Negro education as a mere sop to the Negro race, or perhaps as money entirely thrown away.

I said something like this some years ago to the late Mr. H. H. Rogers and together we devised a plan for giving the matter a fair test. He proposed that we take two or three counties for the purpose of the experiment, give them good schools, and see what would be the result.

We agreed that it would be of no use to build these schools and give them outright to the people, but determined rather to use a certain amount of money to stimulate and encourage the coloured people in these counties to help themselves. The experiment was started first of all in Macon County, Ala., in the fall of 1905. Before it was completed Mr. Rogers died, but members of his family kindly consented to carry on the work to the end of the term that we had agreed upon—that is to say, to October, 1910.

As a result of this work forty-six new school buildings were erected at an average cost of seven hundred dollars each; school terms were lengthened from three and four to eight and nine months, at an average cost to the people themselves of thirty-six hundred dollars per year. Altogether about twenty thousand dollars was raised by the people in the course of this five-year period. Similar work on a less extensive scale was done in four other counties. As a result we now have in Macon County a model public-school system, supported in part by the county board of education, and in part by the contributions of the people themselves.

As soon as we had begun with the help of the coloured people in the different country communities to erect these model schools throughout the county, C. J. Calloway, who had charge of the experiment, began advertising in coloured papers throughout the South that in Macon County it was possible for a Negro farmer to buy land in small or large tracts near eight-months' schools. Before long the Negro farmers not only from adjoining counties, but from Georgia and the neighbouring states, began to make inquiries. A good many farmers who were not able to buy land but wanted to be near a good school began to move into the county in order to go to work on the farms. Others who already had property in other parts of the South sold out and bought land in Macon County. Mr. Calloway informs me that, during the last five years, he alone has sold land in this county to something like fifty families at a cost of $49,740. He sold during the year 1910 1450 acres at a cost of $21,335.

I do not think that any of us realized the full value of this immigration into Macon County until the census of 1910 revealed the extent to which the dislocation of the farming population has been going on in other parts of the state. The census shows, for example, that a majority of the Black Belt counties in Alabama instead of increasing have lost population during the last ten years. It is in the Black Belt counties which have no large cities that this decrease has taken place. Macon County, although it has no large cities, is an exception, for instead of losing population it shows an increase of more than ten per cent.

I think that there are two reasons for this: In the first place there is very little Negro crime and no mob violence in Macon County. The liquor law is enforced and there are few Negroes in Macon County who do not coöperate with the officers of the law in the effort to get rid of the criminal element.

In the second place, Macon County is provided not only with the schools that I have described, but with teachers who instruct their pupils in regard to things that will help them and their parents to improve their homes, their stock, and their land, and in other ways to earn a better living.

When the facts brought out by the census were published in Alabama they were the subject of considerable discussion among the large planters and in the public press generally. In the course of this discussion I called attention, in a letter to the Montgomery *Advertiser*, to the facts to which I have referred.

In commenting upon this letter the editor of The *Advertiser* said:

> The State of Alabama makes liberal appropriations for education and it is part of the system for the benefit to reach both white and black children. It must be admitted that there are many difficulties in properly spending the money and properly utilizing it which will take time and the legislature to correct. The matter complained of in the Washington letter could be easily remedied by the various county superintendents and it is their duty to see that the causes for such complaint are speedily removed.

Negro fathers and mothers have shown intense interest in the education of their children and if they cannot secure what they want at present residences they will as soon as possible seek it elsewhere. We commend Booker Washington's letter on this subject to the careful consideration of all the school officials and to all citizens of Alabama.

The value of the experiment made in Macon County is, in my opinion, less in the actual good that has been done to the twenty-six thousand people, white and black, who live there, than it is in the showing by actual experiment what a proper system of Negro education can do in a country district toward solving the racial problem.

We have no race problem in Macon County; there is no friction between the races; agriculture is improving; the county is growing in wealth. In talking with the sheriff recently he told me that there is so little crime in this county that he scarcely finds enough to keep him busy. Furthermore, I think I am perfectly safe in saying that the white people in this county are convinced that Negro education pays.

What is true of Macon County may, in my opinion, be true of every other county in the South. Much will be accomplished in bringing this about if those schools which are principally engaged in preparing teachers shall turn about and face in the direction of the South, where their work lies. My own experience convinces me that the easiest way to get money for any good work is to show that you are willing and able to perform the work for which the money is given. The best illustration of this is, perhaps, the success, in spite of difficulties and with almost no outside aid, of the best of the Negro medical colleges. These colleges, although very largely dependent upon the fees of their students for support, have been successful because they have prepared their students for a kind of service for which there was a real need.

What convinces me that the same sort of effort outside of Macon County will meet with the same success is that it has in fact met with the same success in the case of Hampton and some other schools that are doing a some-what similar work. On "the educational campaigns" which I have made from time to time through the different Southern States I have been continually surprised and impressed at the interest taken by the better class of white people in the work that I was trying to do. Everywhere in the course of these trips I have met with a cordial, even an enthusiastic, reception not only from the coloured people but from the white people as well.

For example, during my trip through North Carolina in November of 1910, not only were the suggestions I tried to make for the betterment of the schools and for the improve-ment of racial relations frequently discussed and favourably commented upon in the daily newspapers, but after my return I received a number of letters and endorsements from distingushed white men in different parts of the state who had heard what I had had to say.

I was asked the other day by a gentleman who has long been interested in the welfare of the coloured people what I thought the Negro needed most after nearly fifty years of freedom. I promptly answered him that the Negro needed now what he needed fifty years ago, namely, education. If I had attempted to be more specific I might have added that what Negro education needed most was not so much more schools or different kinds of schools as an educational policy and a school system.

In the last analysis, the work of building up such a school system as I have suggested must fall upon the industrial normal schools and colleges which prepare the teacher, because it is the success or failure of the teacher which determines the success of the school. In order to make a beginning in the direction which I have indicated, the different schools and colleges will have to spend much less time in the future than they have in the past in quarrelling over the kind of education the Negro ought to have and devote more time and attention to giving him some kind of education.

In order to accomplish this it will be necessary for these schools to obtain very much larger sums of money for education than they are now getting. I believe, however, if the different schools will put the matter to the people in the North and the people in the South "in the right shape," it will be possible to get much larger sums from every source. I believe the state governments in the South are going to see to it that the Negro public schools get a much fairer share of the money raised for education in the future than they have in the past. At the same time I feel that very few people realize the extent to which the coloured people are willing and able to pay, and, in fact, are now paying, for their own education. The higher and normal schools can greatly aid the Negro people in raising among themselves the money necessary to build up the educational system of the South if they will prepare their teachers to give the masses of the people the kind of education which will help them to increase their earnings instead of giving them the kind of education that makes them discontented and unhappy and does not give them the courage or disposition to help themselves.

In spite of all the mistakes and misunderstandings, I believe that the Negro people, in their struggle to get on their feet intellectually and find the kind of education that would fit their needs, have done much to give the world a broader and more generous conception of what education is and should be than it had before.

Education, in order to do for the Negro the thing he most needed, has had to do more and different things than it was considered possible and fitting for a school to undertake before the problem of educating a newly enfranchised people arose. It has done this by bringing education into contact with men and women in their homes and in their daily work.

The importance of the scheme of education which has been worked out, particularly in industrial schools, is not confined to America or to the Negro race. Wherever in Europe, in Africa, in Asia, or elsewhere great masses are coming for the first time in contact with and under the influence of a higher civilization, the methods of industrial education that have been worked out in the South by, with, and through the Negro schools are steadily gaining recognition and importance.

It seems to me that this is a fact that should not only make the Negro proud of his past, brief as it has been, but, at the same time, hopeful of the future.

CLASSICS *in* BLACK STUDIES SERIES

Martin R. Delany, *The Condition, Elevation, Emigration, and Destiny of the Colored People of the United States* and *Official Report of the Niger Valley Exploring Party*

Anna E. Dickinson, *What Answer?*

Frederick Douglass, *My Bondage and My Freedom*

W. E. B. Du Bois, *Darkwater*

W. E. B. Du Bois, *The Negro*

James L. Smith, *Recollections of a Former Slave*

T. G. Steward, *Buffalo Soldiers: The Colored Regulars in the United States Army*

Booker T. Washington, *My Larger Education: Chapters from My Experience*

Booker T. Washington and Others, *The Negro Problem*

Ida B. Wells-Barnett, *On Lynchings*